PRESIDENTS
on the Net

Gary M. Garfield, Ed.D.
Suzanne McDonough

Good Year Books

An Imprint of Addison-Wesley Educational Publishers, Inc.

Dedication

We dedicate this book to the children who will lead us in the future.

Good Year Books

are available for most basic curriculum subjects plus many enrichment areas. For more Good Year Books, contact your local bookseller or educational dealer. For a complete catalog with information about other Good Year Books, please write:

Good Year Books
1900 East Lake Avenue
Glenview, IL 60025

Acknowledgements appear on page 187.

Book design by Karen Kohn and Associates, Ltd.
Cover illustration by Kelly Alder, copyright © 1999 by the artist.
Interior illustrations by Douglas Klauba.

0-673-36403-8

1 2 3 4 5 6 7 8 9 —ML— 05 04 03 02 01 00 99 98 97

Preface

Presidents on the Net is part of an exciting curriculum combining the best of conventional resources with the new technologies of the Internet. It invites the curious, both teacher and students, to step back in time and visit with the great leaders of our country. It provides an easy-to-understand and user-friendly approach for teachers and students to begin examining these important people in our country's history.

We have made every effort to include only well-established, high-quality presidential and related sites affiliated with credible institutions. We have checked and rechecked the URLs to ensure the quality of this book and the "live" destinations you will seek.

CONTENTS

Introduction   1
How to Use This Book   2
Why This Resource Is Important   3

Part I: Venturing into the World of the Internet: Getting Started   5

Presidents on the Net: Dead Guys?   6
Terms We Should Know Before Our Presidential Visit   7
Now That We Are Connected, How Do We Use It?   8
What Did You Do at School? Today, I Met the President!   9
Invite Your Colleagues and Parents to Meet the Presidents   10
The Presidential Research Center   10
How Do We Work?   11
Getting Organized: Who Moves the Furniture in the White House? 11
The West Wing, the East Wing, or Even a Lab   12
Establishing an Inquisitive Classroom Community   15
Presidential Importance   15
The Integrated Curriculum: Teaching U. S. History Through the
        Presidents   16
Write a Grant: And We Don't Mean Ulysses   16
Have a "Presidential" Press Conference with the Local Media 17
Talk to the President, and You Will Never Be the Same   17

Part II: Presidential Sites and Activities   19

George Washington   20
Site: George Washington   20
Site: Mount Vernon   20
Site: George Washington Papers Home Page   21
Lesson 1: The Qualities of a President   22
Lesson 2: The Beginning of a Tradition   23
Extensions   23

John Adams   24
Site: Inaugural Address   24
Site: The Sedition Act of 1798   24
Site: John Adams   25
Lesson 1: A House Worthy of a President   26
Lesson 2: The Political Party System   27
Extensions   27

Thomas Jefferson   28

   Site: Thomas Jefferson: The Man   28

   Site: Maps and Exploration: Monticello to Lewis and Clark   28

   Site: Jefferson's Home at Monticello   29

   Lesson 1: Inventions   30

   Lesson 2: A Trip Across the Continent   31

   Extensions   31

James Madison   32

   Site: Bill of Rights   32

   Site: War of 1812   32

   Site: James Madison, His Legacy   33

   Lesson 1: Battleship *Constitution*   34

   Lesson 2: Declaration of War   35

   Extensions   35

James Monroe   36

   Site: James Monroe   36

   Site: Home of James Monroe   36

   Site: Monroe Doctrine   37

   Lesson 1: Building a Grand Road   38

   Lesson 2: Was the Monroe Doctrine Equitable?   39

   Extensions   39

John Quincy Adams   40

   Site: Erie Canal   40

   Site: The Amistad Case   40

   Site: Biography of a Statesman   41

   Lesson 1: Seeing Is Believing   42

   Lesson 2: Working on the Erie Canal   43

   Extensions   43

Andrew Jackson   44

   Site: Indian Removal Act of 1830   44

   Site: Alamo de Parras   44

   Site: Jackson's Hermitage   45

   Lesson 1: Point of View   46

   Lesson 2: Nicknames   47

   Extensions   47

Martin Van Buren   48

   Site: Welcome to the Martin Van Buren National Historic Site   48

   Site: Lindenwald   48

   Site: Inaugural Address   49

   Lesson 1: The Panic of 1837   50

   Lesson 2: The Aroostook War,
         Not Really   51

   Extensions   51

William H. Harrison — 52

Site: William Henry Harrison — 52
Site: Battlefield Museum/Tippecanoe County Historical Association — 52
Site: Inaugural Address — 53
Lesson 1: Who Takes the Place? — 54
Lesson 2: Medicine in the 1800s — 55
Extensions — 55

John Tyler — 56

Site: Sherwood Forest, Home of President John Tyler — 56
Site: Annexation of Texas — 56
Site: John Tyler — 57
Lesson 1: Westward Ho — 58
Lesson 2: A Wave of Immigration — 59
Extensions — 59

James K. Polk — 60

Site: James K. Polk — 60
Site: The Gold Rush in California — 60
Site: The U. S.–Mexican War — 61
Lesson 1: Discovering Gold — 62
Lesson 2: The Department of the Interior — 63
Extensions — 63

Zachary Taylor — 64

Site: The Exhumation of President Taylor — 64
Site: Palo Alto Battlefield National Historic Site — 64
Site: Zachary Taylor — 65
Lesson 1: Cinquains About Slavery — 66
Lesson 2: Sing Along with the Forty-Niners — 67
Extensions — 67

Millard Fillmore — 68

Site: Expansion of the Pacific—The Opening of Japan — 68
Site: The Compromise of 1850 — 68
Site: Millard Fillmore — 69
Lesson 1: Japan Has Always Been There — 70
Lesson 2: The Compromise of 1850 Comes Home — 71
Extensions — 71

Franklin Pierce — 72

Site: The Life of Franklin Pierce by Nathaniel Hawthorne, 1852 — 72
Site: The Kansas-Nebraska Act — 72
Site: Franklin Pierce — 73
Lesson 1: The Gadsden Purchase — 74
Lesson 2: Campaign Slogans — 75
Extensions — 75

James Buchanan   76

Site: The Pony Express Station   76
Site: The Dred Scott Decision   76
Site: A Dedicated Public Servant   77
Lesson 1: Dred Scott: A Classroom Trial   78
Lesson 2: Pony Express: A Long Ride for a Short Time   79
Extensions   79

Abraham Lincoln   80

Site: So Many First Facts   80
Site: The Gettysburg Address, November 19, 1863   80
Site: A. Lincoln: Lincoln's Photos and Words   81
Lesson 1: Photographs of Lincoln   82
Lesson 2: Lincoln: A Multimedia Study of a President   83
Extensions   83

Andrew Johnson   84

Site: Impeachment and the Constitution   84
Site: War's Aftermath   84
Site: Andrew Johnson   85
Lesson 1: The Impeachment Process   86
Lesson 2: Alaska, the Foolish Purchase   87
Extensions   87

Ulysses S. Grant   88

Site: Ulysses S. Grant   88
Site: Ulysses S. Grant Network Home Page   88
Site: Ulysses S. Grant Home Page   89
Lesson 1: How Did They Make It Meet?   90
Lesson 2: The Fifteenth Amendment: What Did It Really Mean?   91
Extensions   91

Rutherford B. Hayes   92

Site: Rutherford B. Hayes   92
Site: Inaugural Address   92
Site: Rutherford B. Hayes Presidential Center   93
Lesson 1: Chinese Immigrants and the Development of America   94
Lesson 2: Phone Home . . . to the White House   95
Extensions   95

James A. Garfield   96

Site: James A. Garfield   96
Site: Alexander Graham Bell and the Garfield Assassination   96
Site: James Garfield—Quick Facts   97
Lesson 1: The Bullet   98
Lesson 2: The Assassins   99
Extensions   99

Chester A. Arthur — 100

Site: The History Behind the Man — 100
Site: More Facts — 100
Site: Chester A. Arthur — 101
Lesson 1: My Life Belongs to the People — 102
Lesson 2: Who Owns the President's Personal Papers? — 103
Extensions — 103

Grover Cleveland — 104

Site: Statue of Liberty — 104
Site: Glover Cleveland — 104
Site: Glover Cleveland Home Page — 105
Lesson 1: Election — 106
Lesson 2: A Symbol — 107
Extensions — 107

Benjamin Harrison — 108

Site: Benjamin Harrison — 108
Site: The President Benjamin Harrison Home — 108
Site: Wounded Knee Home Page — 109
Lesson 1: Old Glory — 110
Lesson 2: Ellis Island — 111
Extensions — 111

William McKinley — 112

Site: William McKinley — 112
Site: William McKinley Early Motion Pictures—
    From the American Memory Historical Collections — 112
Site: The Era of William McKinley — 113
Lesson 1: Imperialism and the Philippines — 114
Lesson 2: A Standard That Was Truly Gold — 115
Extensions — 115

Theodore Roosevelt — 116

Site: Theodore Roosevelt — 116
Site: Selected Works of Theodore Roosevelt, New Bartleby Library — 116
Site: Panama Canal — 117
Lesson 1: Mottoes for All Occasions — 118
Lesson 2: The Big Canal — 119
Extensions — 119

William H. Taft — 120

Site: It's Tax Time: The History of the Sixteenth Amendment — 120
Site: Cherry Blossoms in Washington — 120
Site: William H. Taft — 121
Lesson 1: Taxes, Taxes, Taxes — 122
Lesson 2: It's Cherry Blossom Time (or Some Other Tree) — 123
Extensions — 123

Woodrow Wilson   **124**
    Site: From School Master to President   124
    Site: World War I Document Archive   124
    Site: Votes for Women, 1823–1921   125
    Lesson 1: The First War of the World   126
    Lesson 2: The Nobel Prize   127
    Extensions   127

Warren G. Harding   **128**
    Site: Teapot Dome Scandal   128
    Site: American Leaders Speak from the Library of Congress   128
    Site: Warren G. Harding   129
    Lesson 1: The Immigration Reduction Act of 1921   130
    Lesson 2: Meet the President   131
    Extensions   131

Calvin Coolidge   **132**
    Site: Calvin Coolidge   132
    Site: Roaring Twenties   132
    Site: Charles Lindbergh, The Spirit Moved Us All   133
    Lesson 1: They Were the Roaring Twenties   134
    Lesson 2: The *Spirit of St. Louis*   135
    Extensions   135

Herbert C. Hoover   **136**
    Site: It All Came Crashing Down: The Stock Market Crash of 1929   136
    Site: The Great Depression   136
    Site: The Herbert Hoover Presidential Library   137
    Lesson 1: I Lived Through the Depression   138
    Lesson 2: One Dust Bowl—Hold the Rain   139
    Extensions   139

Franklin D. Roosevelt   **140**
    Site: Franklin D. Roosevelt   140
    Site: The History Place: World War II in Europe and the Pacific   140
    Site: Roosevelt and the New Deal   141
    Lesson 1: The New Deal, Relief, and Recovery   142
    Lesson 2: World Leaders of the Time   143
    Extensions   143

Harry S. Truman   **144**
    Site: Harry S. Truman   144
    Site: The City of Hiroshima   144
    Site: Harry S. Truman Library   145
    Lesson 1: Peaceful Use of War's
            Destructive Power   146
    Lesson 2: The United Nations
            for World Peace   147
    Extensions   147

Dwight D. Eisenhower — 148
Site: Dwight D. Eisenhower — 148
Site: Dwight D. Eisenhower Presidential Library — 148
Site: The Montgomery Bus Boycott Page — 149
Lesson 1: The Blacklist — 150
Lesson 2: The Russians Were First — 151
Extensions — 151

John F. Kennedy — 152
Site: Inspiration, Youth, and Humor — 152
Site: John F. Kennedy Assassination Records Collection,
    National Archives and Records Administration — 152
Site: Cuban Missile Crisis — 153
Lesson 1: The Peace Corps — 154
Lesson 2: The Berlin Wall — 155
Extensions — 155

Lyndon B. Johnson — 156
Site: The Lyndon B. Johnson Library and Museum — 156
Site: Challenge for Democracy, Listen to History — 156
Site: Vietnam War — 157
Lesson 1: The Great Society — 158
Lesson 2: The Voting Rights Act — 159
Extensions — 159

Richard M. Nixon — 160
Site: The Facts and Biography — 160
Site: Foreign Policy and the Nixon Years — 160
Site: Watergate — 161
Lesson 1: A Walk on the Wall — 162
Lesson 2: A Man on the Moon . . . or Two — 163
Extensions — 163

Gerald R. Ford — 164
Site: Gerald R. Ford — 164
Site: Gerald Ford Image Gallery — 164
Site: The Gerald Ford Library and Museum — 165
Lesson 1: A President Never Elected — 166
Lesson 2: I Can't Believe It's the Tricentennial — 167
Extensions — 167

James E. Carter, Jr. — 168
Site: Jimmy Carter Library — 168
Site: Camp David Accords: Peace in the Middle East — 168
Site: Jimmy Carter — 169
Lesson 1: Protest and Change — 170
Lesson 2: The Department of Energy — 171
Extensions — 171

Ronald W. Reagan   **172**

   Site: The *Challenger* Accident   172
   Site: The Ronald Reagan Home Page   172
   Site: Ronald Reagan   173
   Lesson 1: From Governor to President   174
   Lesson 2: The Great Communicator   175
   Extensions   175

George H. W. Bush   **176**

   Site: George Bush Biography   176
   Site: George Bush Presidential Library   176
   Site: The Gulf War   177
   Lesson 1: New Government, New Boundaries   178
   Lesson 2: History's Worst Environmental Disaster   179
   Extensions   179

William J. Clinton   **180**

   Site: Current Occupant: Welcome to the White House   180
   Site: President Clinton's Trip to Africa   180
   Site: William Jefferson Clinton   181
   Lesson 1: World Wide Web White House   182
   Lesson 2: The Baby-Boomer President   183
   Extensions   183

Who's Next?   **184**

Election Night Record   **185**

Resources, Journals and Organizations, and Other Places   **186**

Acknowledgements   **187**

Introduction

From the early days of our country, only dignitaries, official government workers, people in physical proximity, the campaign workers, and people the President visits while away from Washington have had access to the President. Few individuals could hope to see the President or obtain firsthand knowledge of his personal views and unique characteristics. Most early Americans never knew what the President actually looked like. Only from the early newspapers, transported across the country by horseback, stagecoach, railroad, and ship, would the literate or those who heard the newspaper being read aloud have an inkling of what the President was actually doing.

Even that news—depending on where the reader was located—could often be three or four months old. As the country expanded both in physical size and population, the influence of the President of the United States increased accordingly.

Today, the new technologies of the Internet and the World Wide Web give all of us the opportunity to peek into the lives and times of all the Presidents of the United States. By using *Presidents on the Net,* we can all have immediate access to the people who have been elected President, their stories, personal history, events, times, and unique qualities and characteristics that influenced the developing republic.

Leave the boat on the Potomac, and cancel your plane reservations. The Presidents, all the Presidents' men, and the First Ladies are awaiting your call on the Information Highway and the World Wide Web. Join us on this journey as "we, the people" access the leaders of this great land.

How to Use This Book

Presidents on the Net is divided into two main sections: (1) the introduction and main text of the book and (2) the Presidents of the United States.

The introductory text is designed to foster a positive climate for venturing into the virtual world of Presidents past and present. It explains the terms, the search, and objective of our study. It looks briefly into schools, organization of classroom learning areas, and the information potential that now belongs to us all. It discusses the strengths and weaknesses of this approach, and it takes the novice or advanced Internet "scholar" to new places and a new way of learning.

The second major section is that of the presidential sites, three for each President, with two related classroom lessons, and three extension activities for further exploration. The Presidents are listed from the earliest to the most recent with space provided to add the next President as the coming election draws near.

For each of the forty-two Presidents, we have identified with a major biographical home page and two additional Internet sites, and we have provided a brief overview of each. (Refer to the table of contents for a complete list.) Accompanying these three presidential sites are two step-by-step classroom lessons that can easily be implemented within the fourth- to eighth-grade classrooms. All lessons have objectives and specify materials, time required, and procedures for implementation.

Finally, three extension activities are provided. These may be used as enrichment with the entire class, with small cooperative groups, or as independent classwork or homework.

Initially, you and your students may wish to do the activities in order. Later, search and explore on your own, conducting research and making personal discoveries about the U. S. Presidents and related issues. New Web sites are constantly being added and existing sites are being further developed. No one can anticipate what will happen in our history, nor what leaders will evolve. As young researchers, our students can be sure that they will have more information to learn about our past, and the opportunity to become more potent in decisions related to our future.

Why This Resource Is Important

Presidents on the Net is part of the new curriculum, combining the best of traditional teaching methods with the contemporary technology of the Internet. Students of this and future generations have opportunities never afforded earlier learners. *Presidents on the Net* removes learning- and physical-resource barriers and provides guaranteed-success learning experiences for teachers and learners. It is a link in a chain of the many learning resources available to teachers. Many teachers will choose to direct or facilitate; others will encourage students to be self-initiating and independent. Regardless of your approach, our goals are clear: to help the learner have successful educational experiences, to make learning exciting, and to advance the possibilities of what our teachers and schools can accomplish.

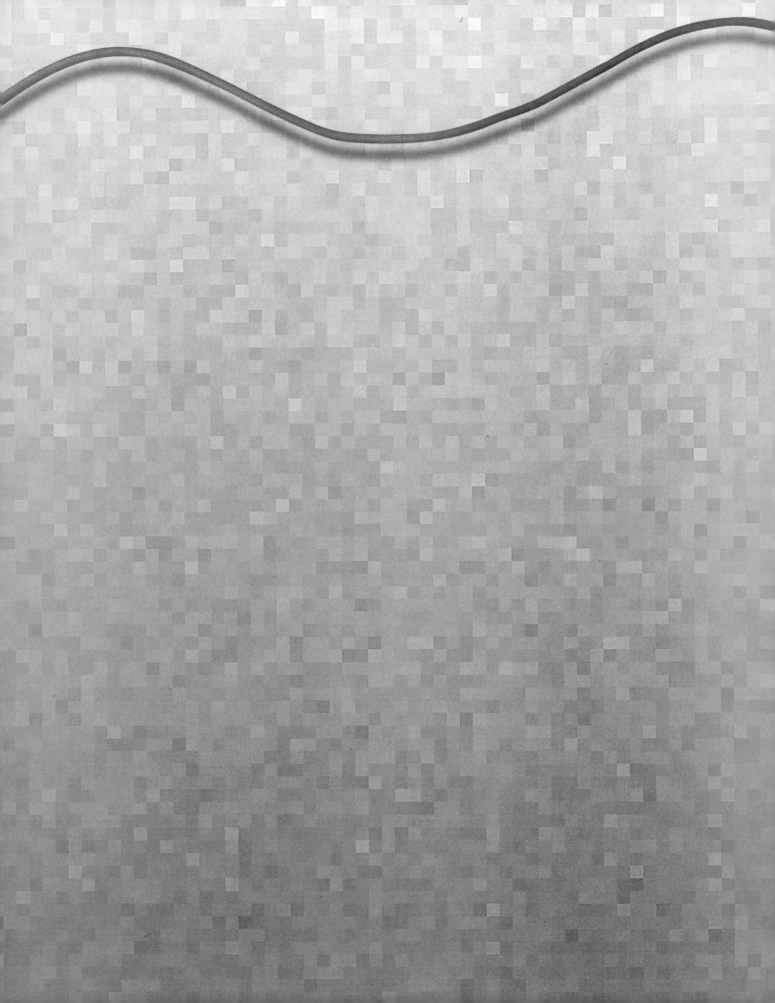

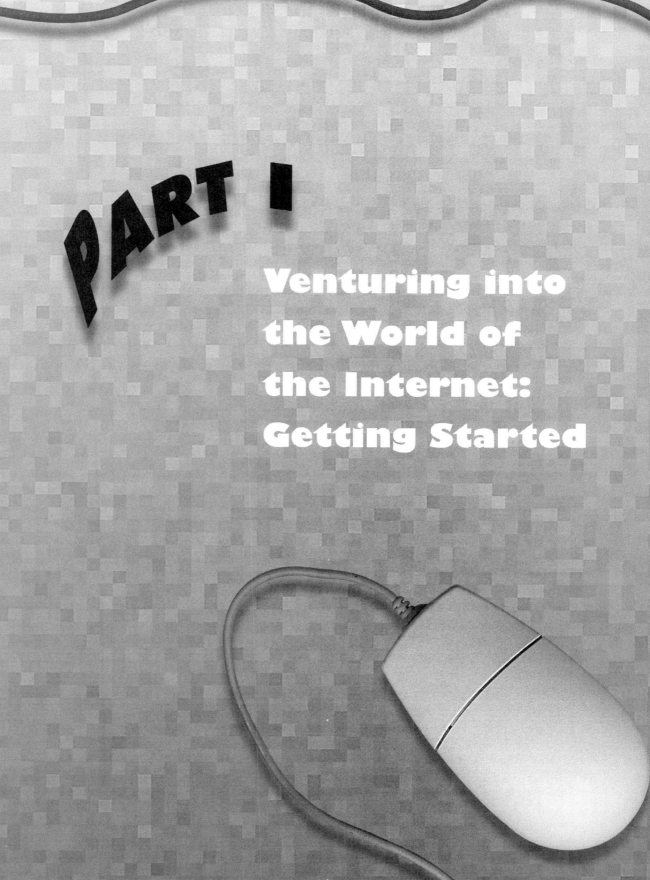

PART I

Venturing into the World of the Internet: Getting Started

Presidents on the Net: Dead Guys?

All children and adults dream of the time machine. How we would love to venture back into history and participate in the events that changed the world. Wouldn't it be exciting to sense the mood of the country during the election of a president in the late 1700s or the mid-1800s or even ten years ago? We don't have a time machine, but we can experience the sights and sounds of the developing Web sites in our important area of study. These multiple-media delivery systems provide the learner with more relevant history than we could ever have obtained with conventional classroom learning resources.

The overriding strengths of *Presidents on the Net* are apparent. Accessibility to presidential collections is available to everyone regardless of factors that have blocked access to resources in the past. Instant access is accomplished with minimal cost, minimal time, convenience of viewing, self-initiating learning, and the opportunity to construct meaning from what we experience.

As materials continue to become available on the Internet, the learning responsibility shifts to the student as to what he or she will construct from this experience. Our only caution when tapping into any resource—whether it be books, online communications, or living experts—is to explore and question each source. We must not accept as truth or fact everything that is in print. Check to see if the sources are reputable, from noted historians, universities, museums, or other institutions that are generally respected. Look for collaboration of sources, and teach your students to do the same. Never just accept information on face value. On the other hand, we should not discount an idea or theory simply because it is different from the mainstream or goes into uncharted territory.

For the teacher, *Presidents on the Net* expands the scope of available resources and personal knowledge. The classroom becomes an infinite reservoir for knowledge. The teacher is no longer responsible for all the answers or limited only to those materials and resources at her/his disposal. We want social studies and history to drive the imagination and energy of our students. We want our students to be part of their own education, not simply recipients.

Come along and find out what *Presidents on the Net* really offers your students. We guarantee that you will not be disappointed, and your students will never be the same.

Terms We Should Know Before Our Presidential Visit

To use *Presidents on the Net*, you need not be a computer programmer, and you do not have to navigate Windows 98, Excel, PowerPoint, or QuarkXPress. All you have to do is follow the instructions and be willing to try new things as your confidence builds.

The terms that follow will help you understand what you are doing and why it is happening. They will also help you understand what the fifth graders are talking about when they break into "computer-ese." These are the most common terms related to searching for and finding information on the World Wide Web. You'll get it quickly. We did!

URLs: URL stands for Uniform Resource Locator. It is simply a one-of-a-kind address for the World Wide Web (WWW) made up of letters, dots, numbers, and/or symbols that give you access to the desired site. With the Internet URL, any Net explorer will be able to find his or her way. In this book, we provide URLs with a brief description for each president. URLs are often too long to remember, so it is important to either cut and paste them or copy them accurately.

Browser: A browser is a graphic interface that aids the user in finding his or her way through cyberspace. In our situation, it is the domicile of each president. With a browser such as Netscape, Microsoft Explorer, America Online Browser, Mosaic, and others, we can easily move about, viewing paintings, photographs, and drawings, as well as reading text in dozens of optional languages.

Search Engines: Search engines are simply indexes that assist the user in finding a specific site of interest. Search engines (InfoSeek, Alta Vista, Excite, Yahoo, etc.) all operate in a similar fashion, but may yield slightly different results. The selection of a particular search engine is generally a matter of personal preference rather than the quality of results. Search engines have a search dialog box, where the user inserts a word or words best describing the topic of the search. Activating the engine with the click of the mouse or the Return key will provide a list from which to choose. The user then selects those titles where the description best matches the desired search.

The URL or Site Box: The URL Dialog Box may display the existing URL or be used as a receptacle to manually insert the letters and symbols of the desired URL. It is usually a long horizontal box just under the tool bar that holds the URL.

Look, Read, and Copy: When inserting a URL in the box, you have to be careful to copy it EXACTLY, or the address will be incorrect and will not reach the desired destination. Thus, look at it closely, read it carefully, and copy it precisely.

Links: Links are simply chains to places related to the topic site that you are viewing. For example, if you are viewing a site about President Thomas Jefferson, you might see a clickable link that takes you to his home in Monticello, or to the Bill of Rights. A quick click on the link, and away you go to the related site.

There are two ways to visit the President of your choice. The easiest method is to copy exactly one of the many URLs (Uniform Resource Locators—for example, http://www.monticello.org/index.html) found under each subject topic in this book. Type it exactly as it appears into the URL or Locator Dialog box on your Web browser, such as the Netscape Navigator, Microsoft Explorer, or AOL browsers. Click "Return," and the navigator will seek the location of the site, bringing it automatically to your screen.

The second method is also easy, but involves a search using one of the many Search Engines. See the preceding "Search Engines" section for a description of this method. As you begin to search more and more (as in learning and practicing any new skill), you will be able to select keywords with greater effectiveness.

Now That We Are Connected, How Do We Use It?

We will make an assumption that your classroom, library, computer lab, or other room or office is connected to the Internet and World Wide Web. If not, your administration or leadership team should be seriously talking about it. If you need help with this, e-mail us at the addresses shown in the Resources section of this book, and we'll pass along some friendly tips. If you are online, you are most likely connected by way of direct cable, wireless, or phone line.

We are all newcomers to telecommunications and the Internet. Of course, some of us have been exploring a little longer, while a few others have even been addressed as "experts." The pace of growth and development of both commercial online services and the Internet has been phenome-nal. While we were once the dispensers of information, we now more often find ourselves facilitating, guiding, and managing our students so that they are able to cross the threshold of content and leap to problem solving and decision making.

The question we are most frequently asked is, "Now that our school is connected to the Internet, what do we do with it that is really meaningful?" A key objective of this book is to answer that question. It is not so much to provide lists of interesting sites, but instead to serve as a model, integrating the study of the U. S. Presidents within our existing curriculum. If teachers begin to embrace the potency of what they are able to discover using this technology, they will realize that the door to the classroom has been flung open in search of answers and more importantly, new questions.

What Did You Do at School? Today, I Met the President!

"Hi, Mom, hi, Dad, hi, Aunt Eleanor! Guess what I did in school today? I met the President of the United States! It was really great."

"Sure honey, that's nice you met the President now in the White House. That's amazing. Good for you."

"No, no, not the current President. I met President Jefferson, and President Lincoln . . . and President Harding . . . and President Truman . . . and President. . . ."

"And so it goes," as a great radio commentator often said. Imagine if your students began the dinner conversation like the above. The amazing digital highway now encourages our young learners to go beyond the classroom walls, seeking information that becomes theirs to explore, to expand upon, and to cherish. These children will meet the Presidents through pictures, written and oral history, written and audio speeches, and even QuickTime movies. Each of the Presidents can be invited into your classroom so that your students will be engaged both in searching and organizing the data, as well as participating in the activities for application.

They will hear it, see it, and actively do things that connect them to these real characters from history.

This is the means by which we learn and thus construct meaning for the event and activity. We must engage our young people in multimodal teaching-learning activities, so that we reach each child on his or her platform of learning. Those who remember something of their educational past remember those activities in which they were "learning engaged," using all of the senses that receive and transmit the event.

Under your tutelage, your students are now ready to "visit the Presidents." They can research and study as you tell them to, or you can set them free to search the corridors of the nation's Capitol, exploring and making discoveries as they travel. That's the exciting part. Stand back and watch your student teams as they travel to Washington, to the battlefields, on foreign missions, or to the meeting rooms of the White House. More than forty presidents, spanning more than two centuries, are all at their fingertips.

Some would call it magic, but for our children in today's schools it is what learning should be. As teachers, we can raise our head proudly and say that we are a part of this exciting and memorable learning. School can be exciting, filled with meaning, adventure, and knowledge.

The Internet has few of the limitations we encounter with the finite volumes of the encyclopedia or the contents of a single computer program. It is infinite in its makeup and possibilities. It allows the student to satisfy his or her inquisitiveness without the teacher assuming the role of "the one who always has the answer." This incredible resource is liberating and powerful for all of us in education.

Invite Your Colleagues and Parents to Meet the Presidents

Our duty as educators is to share with others. As our primary focus, we share with our students. Equally important should be our desire and ability to share our educational strategies with colleagues to help build a better world for all students to learn. The days of the closed classroom door are over. Share your presidential visits and the corresponding classroom projects at faculty meetings, parent meetings, professional conferences, and inservice workshops. It is important to invite our colleagues to join us while we learn about the Presidents on the Net. School will become a wonderful place where amazing things continue to happen.

The Presidential Research Center

Your classroom is being transformed from a traditional place of learning to a "Presidential Research Center." With this new and exciting activity the location deserves a new status. It is important work that your students will undertake, so give the room the name that represents this professional endeavor. Leave the worksheets in the closet and the attitudes at the door, and begin what will transform your young learners into young scholars. Give them the task, set the expectations high, share with them the importance of their work, and watch them as they rise to the occasion. When you introduce a new lesson on the Presidents, reinforce the meaning of what they are doing. Talk in a different way, more "presidential." When you pass by individuals and groups hard at work, writing, reading, doing Internet research, ask them about their work. Let students name their groups in presidential terms, events, slogans, or nicknames. Find music by American composers that give a flavor of this nationalistic historical study.

Transform a section of your room into the "Presidential Corridor" or the "North Wing," or post labels, signs, or posters to set it apart from the conventional areas for activities that will continue in the classroom. Make this learning place a special arena where the youngsters feel that they are unique and where they will flourish and grow. Talk to them, and allow yourself to become excited as they share their accomplishments and new-found knowledge. Encourage them to talk to parents, guardians, and friends about this special learning place. When you, the principal, visitors, or dignitaries visit the room, it will feel different, as there is a heightened level of activity occurring within these walls. You and your students will feel the pride and share the experience.

How Do We Work?

Just as the Presidents and their advisors seldom work in total isolation, your classroom can function in a similar fashion. Certainly students will be doing individual searches, research, and collection of data, but more often than not, you will want your research teams to learn to cooperatively work together. This provides excellent real-world work habits and also maximizes use of the limited hardware and workstations available in most classrooms today.

Thus, dyads, triads, and small cooperative groups seem to be the rule of the house. You can still maintain some of the more traditional roles of groups such as encourager, facilitator, recorder, and others. Groups with such members as advisors, writers, data collectors, and editors all play a pivotal role in this new way of teaching and learning. Using removable, clickable, laminated name tags with roles written on them, such as data collector or editor, indicates the importance of the various roles. As the roles change from search to search, different "role tags" are worn by the student performing each particular role. Your classroom becomes a bustling, professional research center with your students at the hub.

Getting Organized: Who Moves the Furniture in the White House?

Who moves the furniture at the White House? Bet you never asked that question before. What should our classroom look like? How many computers do you need, and how do you decide which children use the computers and when? Just as each of the Presidents had his own style, which carried over into the operation of the White House, so should you do what is consistent with your personality, educational philosophy, and teaching style. There is no one or correct way to organize the learning arena.

We have found that students work well on computers in dyads or small cooperative groups. Peer teams can add a dimension of sharing and excitement to the task. The peer team members can offer necessary assistance in the use of the hardware and software. They can conduct important research related to the Presidents and associated events, eventually constructing theories and offering conclusions. Together, your students will be engaged in constructing and understanding our history.

More and more schools are committed to the classroom as the infinite resource center and are being equipped with multiple computers and workstations. For those with one, two, three, or four computers in your classroom, your well-thought-through method will be the best. Ask others who work in this type of environment. Visit schools where this is the model, post your questions on a bulletin board or user group, attend a computer-using educators' conference in your local area, or check with your county or district office of education. Once you have established your layout, feel comfortable in making adjustments and modifications. Keep in mind that you and your students are engaged in something that is still new, allowing for new ways of teaching and new ways of learning. Demonstrate your high expectations for learning and discovery, and share your excitement about what the students will be accomplishing. You will feel good about your teaching, and they will feel like they have accomplished monumental deeds.

The West Wing, the East Wing, or Even a Lab

Here we have included a few organizational room arrangements for classrooms with from one to four computers. Although computer labs are still prevalent in some settings, our commitment is toward integrating technology into the daily curriculum. In our view, the classroom is the best place for this to happen. This could be accomplished through the classroom computer or a "pod" set between several rooms, which is increasing in popularity.

Some day, when we seriously and radically reorganize our schools, perhaps a lab setting will make sense and will be a natural place for students to freely come and go, doing data gathering and research. Now, however, the lab is often the place where the teacher is usually not in charge, and most often the activities are unrelated to the regular curriculum.

With the new themes presented and a project such as this, the classroom is now a research center and your students are presidential researchers, scholars, or advisors. What a difference a megabyte can make!

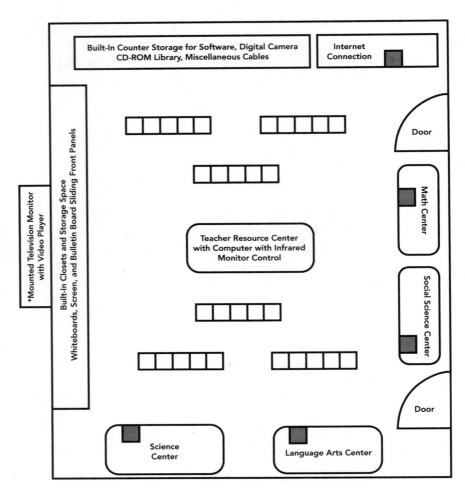

Plan A

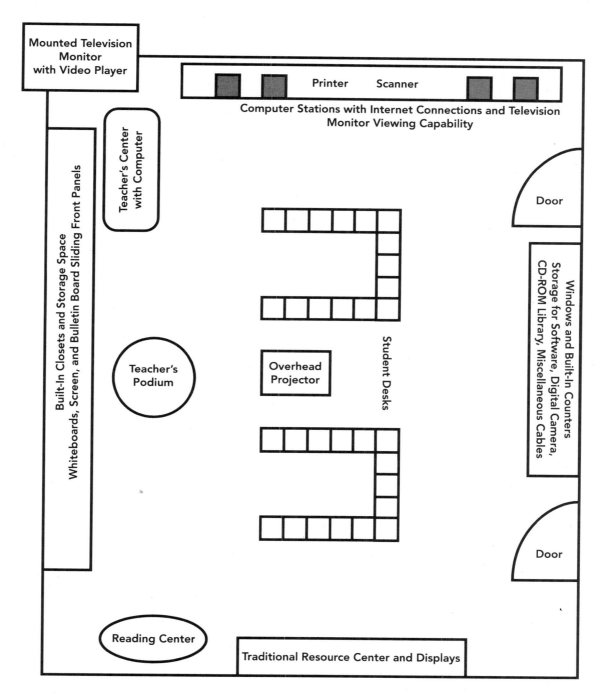

Mounted Television Monitor with Video Player

Printer   Scanner

Computer Stations with Internet Connections and Television Monitor Viewing Capability

Teacher's Center with Computer

Built-In Closets and Storage Space Whiteboards, Screen, and Bulletin Board Sliding Front Panels

Door

Windows and Built-In Counters Storage for Software, Digital Camera, CD-ROM Library, Miscellaneous Cables

Student Desks

Teacher's Podium

Overhead Projector

Door

Reading Center

Traditional Resource Center and Displays

Plan B

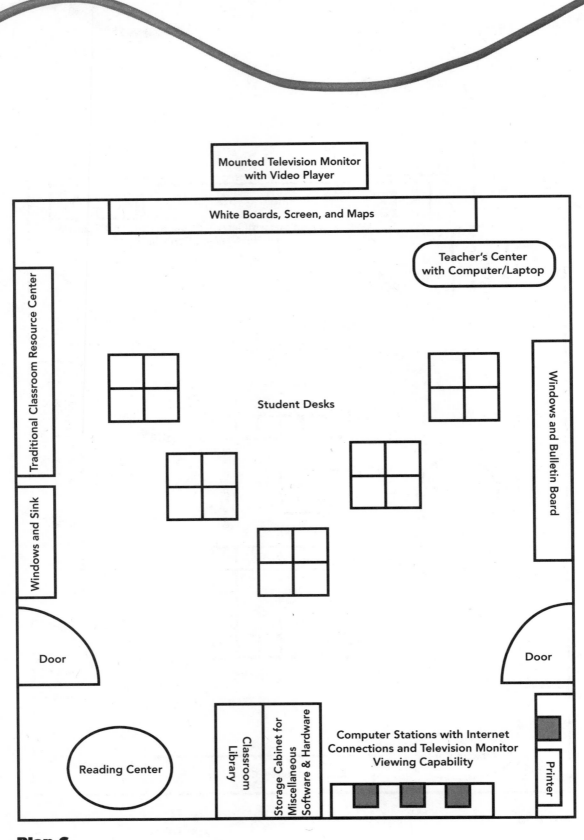

Mounted Television Monitor with Video Player

White Boards, Screen, and Maps

Teacher's Center with Computer/Laptop

Traditional Classroom Resource Center

Windows and Bulletin Board

Student Desks

Windows and Sink

Door

Door

Reading Center

Classroom Library

Storage Cabinet for Miscellaneous Software & Hardware

Computer Stations with Internet Connections and Television Monitor Viewing Capability

Printer

Plan C

Establishing an Inquisitive Classroom Community

It has been well established that a positive feeling of classroom community contributes to effective teaching and meaningful learning. A place where people care about and respect one another contributes to and fosters the cooperative spirit of a positive and productive educational experience. The process of asking questions and seeking resources for information is an exciting classroom endeavor. One of the early criticisms of using computers in the classroom was that children would become isolated from classmates and teacher. But students share their exciting discoveries with each other, expanding the inquiry into a variety of associated learning tasks. These include further online research, conventional library work, writing, literature, discussions and debate, decision making and problem solving. Through the expanded associated activities, the children are again constructing new meaning for the events occurring in this new classroom community. *Presidents on the Net* offers opportunities for engagement in this special community. The history of the Presidents and all the associated information is always open to interpretation. Our students will look at some events at face value (Lincoln signing the Emancipation Proclamation) and others in the context of the time they occurred (Jefferson as a slave owner). These appropriate and scholarly discussions will positively reinforce the developing intellectual classroom community.

Presidential Importance

Everyone considers what the President does as important work. So, if we are committed to researching the Presidents' work, that too should be considered important. If we treat students' work as important, they will think of it as important. When a parent or teacher has reasonably high expectations of students' work, students will generally perform at the level of the expectation. Conversely, if the expectations are low, or the work is deemed unimportant, students will behave accordingly. Our presidential study is important! Our students are young historians and scholars embarking on a new journey to view history through the Internet. As teachers, we must spend time talking about the important work we are all doing. Treat your young scholars with respect and dignity, and ask them often, "How is the work progressing?" "What have you discovered about the President?" "Why is it important?" and "Who is it important to?" Although you hold the reins, it will not be long before the students take the lead. When visitors come to your class, the children will be working in large groups, small groups, and as individuals, but will always be engaged in meaningful work. The visitors will be impressed, observing this research arena, but most important, your students will feel a sense of immense personal pride in their important accomplishments. They are learning, and they are growing.

The Integrated Curriculum: Teaching U. S. History Through the Presidents

We do not mandate a particular way to teach this subject. Some of our colleagues will teach one President at a time, or the Presidents in a particular period in our history, or random Presidents as the mood moves them. One very effective way of thematic teaching is to build your U. S. history curriculum around the presidential study. Each week study a different President with the rich and interesting associated topics and engaging activities surrounding that particular time in history. The President becomes a hat rack or magnet to tie all the other interesting things that occurred during that time. You will be surprised how much your students will remember and how important it will seem. Thus, teach and connect the President with the historical events of the period. Examine the art, music, and social issues in America and abroad. Allow the students to give meaning to the study.

Write a Grant: And We Don't Mean Ulysses

Perhaps your study of the U. S. Presidents will require some additional support. Think about the resources that abound in and around your school. Small grants, often thought to be outside the realm of the regular teacher, are often available for the asking. Sure, you can apply for the grants everyone knows about, like those sent to the county office or through the state department of education. You can also seek out grants from organizations that are less known. Check the technology resource pages on the Internet, which often list resources for grants up to $5,000 for creative classroom ideas integrating technology. Check with local corporations and businesses who want to and often need to support local projects for political, social, and tax reasons. All you have to do is ask. The worst that can happen is that you end up with the same bottom line that you had before you started. Don't worry if you have not done this before. The criteria for the small grants are very explicit, and you usually will only have to write a couple of pages responding to a set of questions. You and a colleague will enjoy the process, and it's all the more fun if you land the big one!

Have a "Presidential" Press Conference with the Local Media

What goes better with the study of the Presidents than a made-to-order media event? Of course, we have all seen press conferences where reporters crowd into the press room and the President or his press secretary fields questions related to the events of the day. We have discovered that the local news media respond well to the teacher's request for event coverage, just like in Washington, D.C. Simply telephone the education desk of the local newspaper (they all have them) and let them know of the special event that will be occurring in your classroom. Be sure to tell them that it is also a good photo opportunity, known as a "photo op" in the trade. Your presidential study or accompanying activities will make good news and a great visual for the newspaper. Topics about government and civics education are always popular. Be sure to write a summary ahead of time with the relevant facts about your project. Include a few choice personal quotes (yours) so the reporters will get it right when they return to the newspaper office. Watch the newsstands the next day, and savor the few minutes of media fame. Be sure to send a copy of the article to the superintendent and the principal.

Talk to the President, and You Will Never Be the Same

Learning translates to change of behavior. The students are less dependent, and they approach problem solving and decision making in very different ways. They appear more mature and seem to possess a secret about the world of information and their personal power in learning. It is exciting to see this transformation as our students evolve in the infinite world of information and knowledge. The students who are in your class and engaged in this journey with the U. S. Presidents on the Net will never again be satisfied with what was the norm in education. As your students become part of this new way of learning and you become a part of the new way of teaching, none of you will ever be the same.

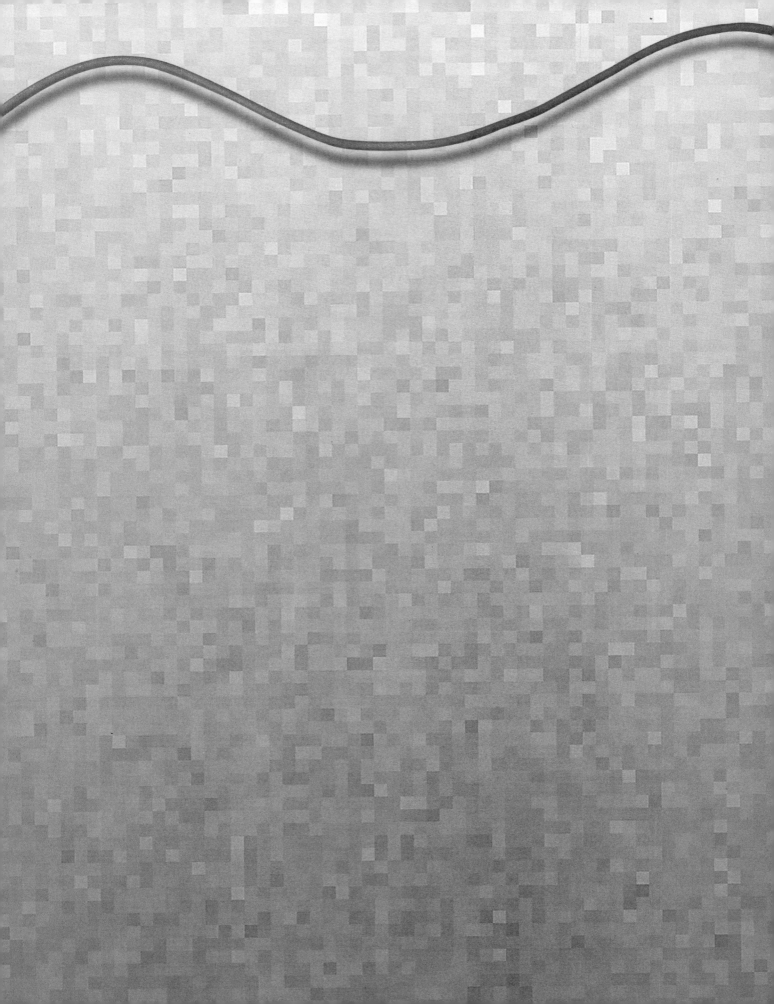

PART 2

Presidential Sites and Activities

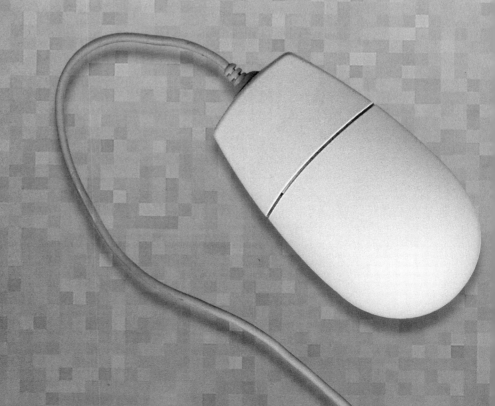

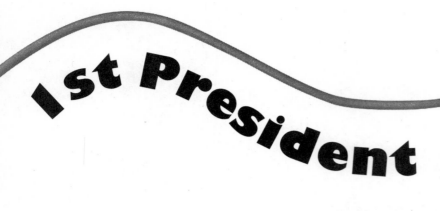

1st President

George Washington
1789 – 1797

George Washington became the first President of a vibrant nation struggling for independence. President Washington was a gentleman who with the greatest of personal integrity set the standard for all who would some day lead this young nation.

George Washington

http://www.ipl.org/ref/POTUS/gwashington.html

Although everyone knows that George Washington was the "Father of His Country," few know about his education, religion, occupation, or political party. This site takes you from his personal data to all the facts about his election, members of his Cabinet, and highlights from his presidency.

Mount Vernon

http://www.mountvernon.org/

You might call Mount Vernon the "First House for the First Family." Join the virtual tour of Washington's Mount Vernon, the estate, and gardens.

THE PAPERS OF GEORGE WASHINGTON

G Washington

Papers of George
Washington
Series Information
Project News
Selected Documents
Selected Articles
Indexes
Staff Directory
Letterpress Volumes
Search the Washington
Papers Website
Site Awards and Links
Contact the Washington
Papers
Language Translator

George and Martha Washington

George Washington Papers Home Page

http://www.virginia.edu/gwpapers/

We search the attic and the basement for old letters, journals, and documents in hopes of discovering a special document from the past. This site shares historic letters and documents written by George Washington. These materials are now available not only to scholars, but to any American who can point and click.

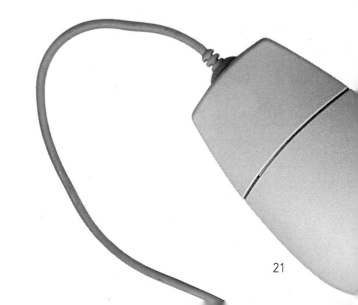

21

The Qualities of a President

As the new government began to form, the nation looked for a leader whose past accomplishments showed strength, character, and merit. As Commander-in-Chief of the Continental Army during the Revolutionary War, George Washington proved himself to be a capable leader. In 1789, Washington took the oath of office as the first President of the United States.

Objective

Students will identify and list ten qualities an individual should possess in order to be President of the United States.

Time Required

45 minutes

Materials

• Posterboard
• Markers
• Books and stories about the life of George Washington
• Internet access

Procedure

As individuals, or in cooperative groups, have students research the life of George Washington using both traditional and technological resources. Instruct the students to focus on the events in his life that provide insight into his character.

Dispel the myths that are often taught, and focus on the facts. Events that may provide insight are

• Washington's leadership as he presided over the Constitutional Convention
• Washington's military career and his involvement in the Revolutionary War
• Washington's ability to select and appoint people to head departments in the government

Bring the class together as one large group. Collectively generate a list outlining the qualities George Washington demonstrated in his life that enabled him to lead the new nation. Ask students to justify their responses. Narrow the list to Washington's top ten qualities.

As an extension of this lesson, create a Venn diagram comparing the present-day President to George Washington. What character traits do they have in common? What traits are different? Do the character traits of Presidents differ because the society each lived in was different? Ponder the answers to these and to student-generated questions.

The Beginning of a Tradition

Our images of our first President come to us from the portraits painted by artists of his time. Talented masters attempted to capture the essence and dimension of prominent individuals and to transfer this onto the flat canvas. Today every schoolchild can recognize the first President of the United States based on these portraits. Leading portrait painters of the era were Gilbert Stuart and Charles Willson Peale. George Washington sat for both artists. It is Stuart's unfinished portrait of Washington that was used for the etching of the one dollar bill. Other artists, such as Emanuel Leutze, painted Washington years after his death. The famed painting "Washington Crossing the Delaware," created in 1851, hangs in the Metropolitan Museum of Art in New York City.

Objective

Following a study of the famous portraits of George Washington, students will create their own self-portraits.

Time Required

1 1/2 hours

Materials

- White drawing paper
- Pencil, color pencil, crayon, or watercolor paint
- Paintbrushes
- Mirrors
- Research books
- Internet access

Procedure

As a group, view and discuss the various images of Washington presented in the paintings. These can be found in traditional resources, such as art books, history books, and art posters. If technology and Internet access is available, download the images to the computer and display them on a large television monitor in the classroom. Discuss the different feature in each painting that gives the viewer insight into the person being portrayed. Take note of the fashion styles of the times, the use of light on the face, and any focal points within the painting that make it unique.

Following the group discussion, give each student a piece of white drawing paper. Using crayons, markers, colored pencils, or watercolors, students will create their own self-portraits. Have each student look at himself or herself in the mirror. Focus on the hairstyles, use of makeup and jewelry, and clothing of the present day, and include these in the individual portraits. The students can then add a background that reflects the places, people, and things in their lives. Mount the finished portraits, and display for all to enjoy.

Extensions

1. Students will write a letter to a relative in Europe telling about the young nation and its new leader, George Washington. Use parchment paper and a calligraphy pen to present the document in an authentic fashion.

2. During the time of George Washington, agriculture was the primary industry in the United States. Grow a classroom garden. Assign maintenance tasks and responsibilities to each member of the class. When the crops are cultivated, enjoy a vegetarian feast.

3. *The Meta Given's Cookbook* proudly features "George Washington Gingerbread." Locate the recipe at the local library. Gather the ingredients, and bring them into the classroom. Supply the students with measuring spoons, spatulas, bowls, and measuring cups. Have the students mix together all the ingredients. Bake in the cafeteria oven, and serve warm with a dollop of whipping cream. Even George would say it is the best he ever ate!

2nd President

John Adams
1797 - 1801

Before being elected President, John Adams served under George Washington as the first Vice-President of the United States. During his administration, the government moved from Philadelphia to Washington, D.C., and he was the first President to inhabit the White House. Adams was integral in planning the Revolution, and he was a signer of the Declaration of Independence.

Inaugural Address

http://www.cc.columbia.edu/acis/bartleby/inaugural/pres15.html

While none of us could be in the center of government on Saturday morning, March 4, 1797, we can still read Adams's words of reflection about the struggling nation and his personal view of constitutional behavior.

The Sedition Act of 1798

http://www.law.uoknor.edu/hist/sedact.html

Become an insider as you learn about the perceived need for the Sedition Act and the imperatives it established for a country still struggling for existence. Your class can debate the issues presented in this powerful law of 1798.

John Adams
Second President 1797–1801

[Abigail Smith Adams]

Fast Fact: John Adams, a shaper of the revolution, saved his Nation from war with France.

Inaugural Address

John Adams

http://www.whitehouse.gov/WH/glimpse/presidents/html/ja2.html

After two terms as Vice-President, John Adams assumed the reins of government in the new nation, and had to focus much of his wisdom and attention on foreign affairs with England and France. Join Adams for his inaugural address, familiar quotations, and, of course, the many interesting facts related to the second President of the United States.

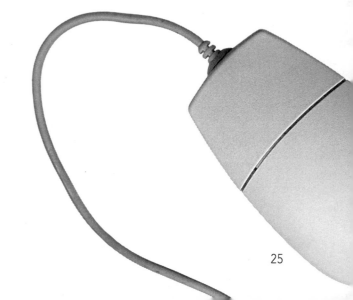

A House Worthy of a President

Although George Washington selected the site for the present-day White House, John Adams was the first President to live there. Begun in 1792, the structure was still unfinished when Adams and his family took up residence in 1800. Adams wrote to his wife, "Before I end my letter, I pray Heaven to bestow the best of Blessings on this House and all that shall hereafter inhabit it. May none but honest and wise Men ever rule under this roof."

Objective

Following a discussion about the White House, students will create and design a house suitable for a President.

Time Requirement

1 hour

Materials

- Drawing paper
- Rulers or metric sticks
- Pencils, markers, and colored pencils

Procedure

Students will research the history of this famous building. Access the White House Web site to learn about the structure and the people and events that shaped the history of the White House. Discover the changes and improvements made to the White House as each President and his family took up residence for the term of office.

Following the classroom discussion, instruct the students to design a new home for the President. Students will develop both a floor plan and a sketch of the front of the house. Suggest that they select a new location for the White House that would be conducive to a modern President's life-style. Research current trends in architecture, and include these in the new design. Remind the students to include modern technologies and innovations in the blueprints. The design should include space for official government offices, family life, recreation, entertainment, and high-tech communications.

As an extension to the activity, students will construct small-scale models of their buildings.

The Political Party System

The national leaders who wrote the U. S. Constitution had hoped to avoid divisiveness within political parties. However, during George Washington's administration, party division began to occur. Those with the Federalist belief in a strong centralized national government united around John Adams. The Democratic-Republican party, or Jeffersonians, shared the views of Thomas Jefferson, who favored minimum government and the interests of the working class. The transformation of these factions eventually resulted in the two major parties of today, the Democratic Party and the Republican Party.

Objective

Students will debate issues based on a political party's platform.

Time Requirement

Two sessions of 1 hour each

Materials

- Internet access
- Newspapers
- Index cards
- Writing materials
- Podium
- Campaign materials from local, state, or national political parties

Procedure

Divide the students into two or three groups. Each group will be assigned to collect information about the platforms of the major political parties that reflect their diverse outlooks and interests. Visit official headquarters to collect information about the parties' candidates and issues. Contact and interview the elected officials in the community for further insight.

Give the students a topic to debate. This should be an issue that could affect their local, state, or national community. Allow each group an equal amount of time to comment and share their viewpoints. The teacher may serve as facilitator. Invite other classes to hear the arguments and vote on the issues.

Extensions

1. The Library of Congress was established in 1800. Where once only a few scholars were privileged to use the large collection, today anyone with a computer and Internet access can view and research the massive collections that are available online. Encourage your students to browse through this impressive national library.

2. Congress established a separate Department of the Navy in 1798 after launching two magnificent tall ships the previous year. The ships were the U.S.S. *Constitution* and the U.S.S. *Constellation*. These two vessels made up the core of the Navy's fighting force. Have your students examine these historical ships via the Internet. They can also view some of the many modern ships of today's Navy. Do they see any similarities?

3. The federal government moved from Philadelphia to its current location in Washington, D.C., in 1800. Why would the government need or want to move? Explore these two cities for evidence that will support your response.

3rd President

Thomas Jefferson
1801 – 1809

Thomas Jefferson, the author of the Declaration of Independence, was a man of many talents. He was a diplomat, political thinker, inventor, and, of course, President of the United States. During his presidency, the United States doubled in size with the Louisiana Purchase in 1803.

Thomas Jefferson: The Man

http://www.whitehouse.gov/WH/glimpse/presidents/html/tj3.html

Discover Thomas Jefferson, the third President of the United States. Learn about the man and his remarkable life. Attend his inauguration—or at least read the text of his speech—or flip through the many famous quotations from this great statesman. This site links dozens of related sites, including those that expand our understanding of Jefferson, leader of a young nation.

Maps and Exploration: Monticello to Lewis and Clark

http://www.lib.virginia.edu/exhibits/lewis_clark/home.html

Find your way from Monticello to the Pacific Northwest as we discover these interesting sites with links to maps of the New World and the continent being explored by the Lewis and Clark expedition. As mapping and map reading are essential within the elementary school curriculum, this is the perfect site to search.

Jefferson's Home at Monticello

http://www.monticello.org/index.html

Home is where you hang your hat, or in this case, your coat, boots, clock, and paintings. Monticello provides an exciting and fascinating glimpse into the daily life of Thomas Jefferson. Many of his inventions and innovations can be seen throughout the house. The stables under the residence, the slave quarters on the grounds, and the massive vegetable garden teach us about the life and legend of this remarkable individual.

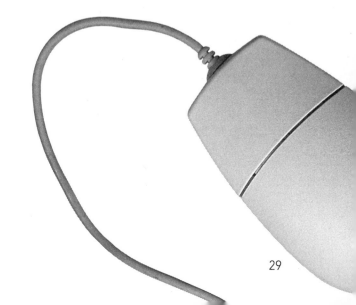

Inventions

Thomas Jefferson proved himself to be not only a political genius, but also a creative inventor. Take your students on a virtual tour of Monticello to discover the inventive ingenuity of one of our most prominent founding fathers. Discover the fascinating inventions he created for his home and his environment.

Objective

In cooperative groups, students will design and construct an invention that improves upon a functional need within the classroom environment.

Time Required

Two sessions of 1 hour each

Materials

- Drawing paper
- Rulers
- Pencil, crayons, and/or markers
- Construction paper
- Glue and/or tape
- Yarn, string, rubber bands

Procedure

Instruct the students to identify places and things in their own classroom environment that might work better or be designed differently to function better. Discuss and brainstorm ideas for inventions that would be applicable to the classroom environment. Possible suggestions may include

- An organizational insert for the desk to keep the messiest students organized
- A desktop pencil-and-pen holder that would prevent items from falling on the floor
- A system to keep glue bottles and marker caps secured properly to prevent drying out
- A way to remove pencil shavings from the floor
- A device to prevent backpacks from falling off the chair or hook
- A device to keep books from falling out of an open backpack (since children don't seem to want to use the zipper)
- A device to prevent the classroom map from being pulled down too far and jamming
- A method to determine when the paper towel dispenser is almost, but not quite, empty

In cooperative groups, students should select a topic for change or improvement and design an invention to meet one of the classroom needs. Ask students to first put their plans on paper and create a schematic drawing showing the design and its functional outcome. They should be sure to include information on size and dimension, ease of use, and placement in the room. Use only those materials provided in the classroom, if possible.

Following the completion of the inventions, allow ample time for the students to share and demonstrate their creations to the entire group. Implement these within the classroom.

A Trip Across the Continent

The expedition of Meriwether Lewis and William Clark between the years of 1804 and 1806 documented the vast territory between the Mississippi River and the Pacific Coast. President Jefferson wanted to confirm the existence of the Northwest Passage or water route connecting the East and West Coasts. Traveling thousands of miles over uncharted territory, Lewis and Clark mapped and journalized their historic adventure, thus opening the West to the nation.

Objective

Following a study of the Core of Discovery, the students will create a salt-and-flour relief map of the territory Lewis and Clark explored in their famed expedition.

Time Required

Three sessions of 1 hour each

Materials

- Maps showing the territory explored by Lewis and Clark
- Flour
- Salt
- Water
- Tempera paint
- Cardboard

Procedure

In cooperative groups, students should research the expedition of Lewis and Clark. On a map of the United States, plot the route they took as they traveled west. Transfer the outline of the map onto a piece of cardboard.

Provide each group with the following ingredients to create the salt-and-flour dough:

- 2 cups of flour
- 1 cup of salt
- 1/2 cup of water

Mix the flour and the salt together. Slowly add the water until the mixture is thick enough to hold a shape.

Spread a thin layer of dough on the surface of the map. Using small pieces, begin to build up the map to create areas that represent higher land elevations. Allow the map to dry for one or two days. Using tempera paint, students can highlight the major geographic sites explored by the expedition. These should include the Mississippi River, the Missouri River, the Rockies, the Continental Divide, and the Snake and Columbia Rivers.

Extensions

1. In 1803, the land acquired through the Louisiana Purchase extended from the Mississippi River to the Rocky Mountains, more than 800,000 square miles. It was purchased for about fifteen million dollars. Have students calculate the cost per square mile and the cost per acre. Research what the cost would be at today's land values.

2. Noah Webster began his work on an English language dictionary in 1800. First published in 1806, *Webster's Dictionary* is still in use as a major resource for writing. Have the students look up words in a *Webster's Dictionary* that would describe Thomas Jefferson and his contributions to the nation.

3. Connect online to the Library of Congress and download information on how to obtain a U. S. patent for an invention.

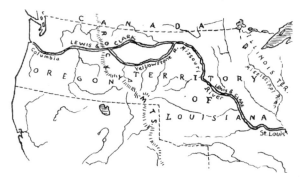

4th President

James Madison
1809 - 1817

James Madison is often referred to as the "Father of the Constitution." He objected, saying that the Constitution was not "the offspring of a single brain, but the work of many heads and many hands." As a member of Congress, Madison helped frame the Bill of Rights.

War of 1812

http://www.multied.com/1812/

The War of 1812 is one of the forgotten wars fought by the United States. Although it lasted more than two years, it ended in a stalemate. The war had no winners, and enthusiasm for participation never materialized. This site chronicles this unusual conflict.

Bill of Rights

http://www.netins.net/showcase/ wizardave/soapbox/basics/billrts.htm

As James Madison was indeed the "Father of the Constitution," it seems only appropriate to include the Bill of Rights and other quotations from the honorable President Madison.

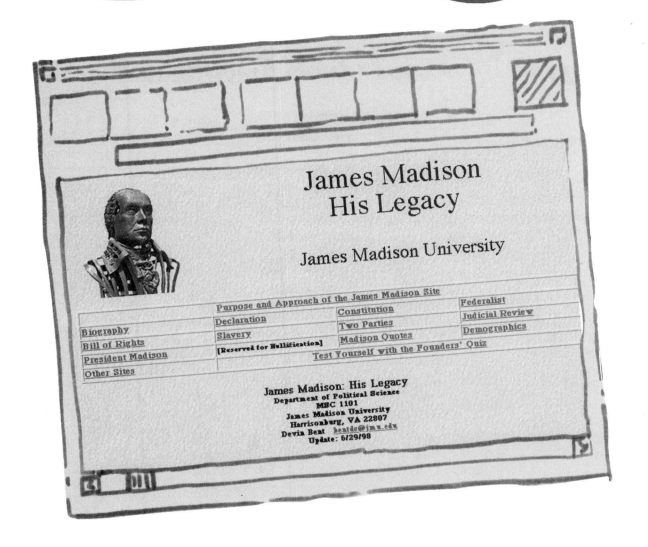

James Madison
His Legacy

James Madison University

Biography	Purpose and Approach of the James Madison Site		Federalist
	Declaration	Constitution	Judicial Review
Biography	Slavery	Two Parties	Demographics
Bill of Rights	[Reserved for Nullification]	Madison Quotes	
President Madison			
Other Sites	Test Yourself with the Founders' Quiz		

James Madison: His Legacy
Department of Political Science
MSC 1101
James Madison University
Harrisonburg, VA 22807
Devin Bent bentdc@jmu.edu
Update: 6/29/98

James Madison, His Legacy

http://www.jmu.edu/polisci/madison/JM.ht

"James Madison, His Legacy" contains writings, documents, and events from his influential presidency. This site is a treasure trove of background information about the man who is known as the "Father of the Constitution."

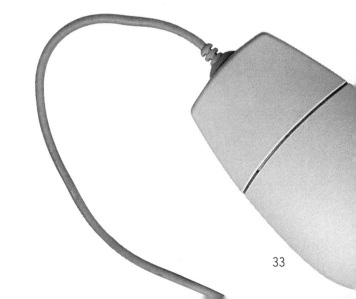

33

Battleship Constitution

The U.S.S. *Constitution* was one of the first frigates of the U. S. Navy. First launched in 1797, the warship remained active until 1815. After winning battles in the War of 1812, she was saved from the scrap heap in 1830 largely due to public interest brought about by the poem "Old Ironsides" by Oliver Wendell Holmes.

Objective

Following the reading of Oliver Wendell Holmes's poem "Old Ironsides," students will create an illustration of the U.S.S. *Constitution.*

Time Required

1 hour

Materials

- A copy of "Old Ironsides" by Oliver Wendell Holmes
- Drawing paper
- Pencils, markers, colored pencils
- Rulers

Procedure

Read the famous poem "Old Ironsides" aloud to the class. Then have students access the Internet and traditional resources for information and photographs of the U.S.S. *Constitution.* Ask students to study the ship and create an illustration. The illustrator may either draw a picture of the famed frigate as she appeared in battle, or as she is today, anchored at dock.

Using a computer or word processor, type and print out a copy of the poem. Be sure to use an eye-catching font. Mount the poem on a bulletin board. Surround the poem with the students' drawings for an impressive display.

Declaration of War

The United States and Great Britain fought from 1812 to 1815 in what we call the War of 1812. Madison moved cautiously. When he finally conceded to public pressure and asked Congress to declare war, it took another seventeen days of debate for the declaration to be passed.

Objective

Students will list the steps necessary for the United States to declare war.

Time Required

45 minutes

Materials

- A copy of the U. S. Constitution
- Encyclopedias
- Internet access
- Butcher paper
- Markers

Procedure

Students will discover that war is not a simple choice left to the judgment of one individual. Collect information on the process and steps necessary for the United States to declare war on another nation. Discover if the United State always declares war before sending troops into battle. Discuss the conflicts a President must ponder when making such an important recommendation.

Extensions

1. As an inquiry lesson, students will explore the origin of "Uncle Sam." (Hints: The War of 1812, a man by the name of Samuel Wilson, and stamped barrels.)

2. Francis Scott Key was inspired by events related to the War of 1812 when he wrote the words that would later become known as "The Star-Spangled Banner." After students have read or sung the poem, discuss why they think it became the national anthem in 1931.

3. Dolley Madison, wife of President Madison, is often considered to be one of the most extraordinary women in U. S. history. One story tells of her courage when fleeing the White House as the British marched on Washington. She is credited with saving some very important items. List those items. Ask students to think about the one thing they might take from their own homes if asked to flee quickly. (Emphasize that it is more important to get out than to save possessions.) Have them give reasons for their choices.

5th President

James Monroe
1817 - 1825

James Monroe is remembered for the Monroe Doctrine, which essentially warned European countries not to interfere with the domestic affairs of free nations in the Western Hemisphere. His presidency capped more than forty years of public service that began during the Revolutionary War.

Home of James Monroe

http://pulex.med.virginia.edu/highland/index.html

Ash Lawn-Highlands was home to James Monroe from 1799–1826. It filled a sprawling 3,500 acres at the time Monroe lived there. Today's visitor on the Information Highway can learn about the history of the house, read a brief biography of James Monroe, and view pictures of the art, rooms, plantation, and gardens. Be sure to "listen and look" for the colorful peacocks.

James Monroe

http://www2.whitehouse.gov/WH/glimpse/presidents/html/jm5.html

James Monroe spent nearly fifteen weeks traveling from state to state learning about the people and the country. The visitor to this site will travel with Monroe through an extraordinary array of personal and presidential accomplishments. Follow him from growth and protection of the United States to weddings in the White House. James Monroe was the last of the Presidents who had served as an officer in this country's Revolutionary War.

THE MONROE DOCTRINE

President James Monroe

Monroe Doctrine

http://www.grolier.com/presidents/
ea/side/mondoc.html

One of the best-known accomplishments of the Monroe administration was the formation of the Monroe Doctrine. Visit these documents and learn how notice was given to our European relatives to forgo any further colonization in America.

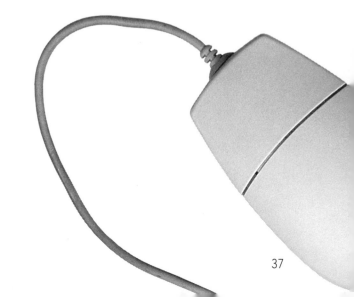

Lessons for Learning

Building a Grand Road

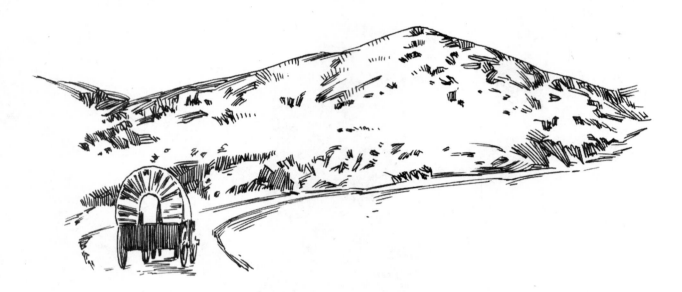

The Cumberland Road, or, as it become known, the National Road, was a precursor to our modern highways. Students will learn about the Cumberland Road and then design and construct their own road. Students will also learn how to read both topographical maps and relief maps.

Objective

Students will design a road that crosses some obstacles, such as rivers, valleys, and mountains.

Time Required

1 hour

Materials

- Three overlay transparencies, created by you or purchased at a local school supply store
- Nonpermanent fine-tipped marking pens
- Overhead projector

Procedure

Give groups of two students each a work problem map, Transparency 1, showing an area to be traversed by a newly constructed road. Transparency 2 will indicate clearly a variety of geographical terrains. Using an overlay, Transparency 3, students will plot the most reasonable location for the new road.

Next, each team will share its recommendations, which may be professionally challenged by classmates. To archive the drawings, overlay the three transparencies and mount them over lightly colored construction paper. Label them, add students' names, and display.

Was the Monroe Doctrine Equitable?

On December 2, 1823, President James Monroe presented a message to Congress that is still the foundation of American foreign policy. The Monroe Doctrine, as it later became known, was a statement that outlined United States' policy against further colonization of the Americas and established the nation's role as a global power with influence and interests beyond its boundaries.

Objective
Students will study and debate the equity of the Monroe Doctrine in light of current United States policies in or near to foreign soil.

Time Required
1 hour of research and planning
1 hour of presentation

Materials
• Historical background on the Monroe Doctrine
• Internet access
• Library access
• Writing materials

Procedure
Following the introduction to the Monroe Doctrine, have students compare the intent of the Doctrine in 1823 to the "nondeclared war" presence of the United States in various parts of the world through history. Ask them to present their insights and positions related to this issue.

Extensions
1. The Monroe period became known as the "Era of Good Feeling" because of national optimism, expansion, and growth. What times in recent history could be compared to the "Era of Good Feeling"? Class teams can research this area and compare findings.

2. Write a speech that warns foreign countries that their occupation or presence on our lands will not be tolerated.

3. Obtain maps from the auto club showing the Eastern United States, and see if students can plot the original Cumberland Road.

6th President

John Quincy Adams
1825 - 1829

John Quincy Adams became the only son of a President who himself was elected to the presidency. A graduate of Harvard College, Adams served as Minister to the Netherlands and later Minister to Russia. He served under James Monroe and as Secretary of State helped craft the Monroe Doctrine. As President, Adams urged the United States to take a leading role in the development of the sciences and the arts, the establishment of roads and canals, and the preservation of public lands.

The Amistad Case

http://www.nara.gov/education/teaching/amistad/home.html

After his presidency ended, John Quincy Adams eloquently defended abducted Africans intended for the slave trade bound for the Americas. This legal battle and triumph become known as the Amistad Case. Adams's defense focused on their rights to fight to regain their lost freedom.

Erie Canal

http://www.history.rochester.edu/canal/

John Quincy Adams took an active role in encouraging trade and commerce during his term as President. Thus, it was befitting that the Erie Canal became a new route for shipping and trade. Sail along this site to learn about this unique seaway.

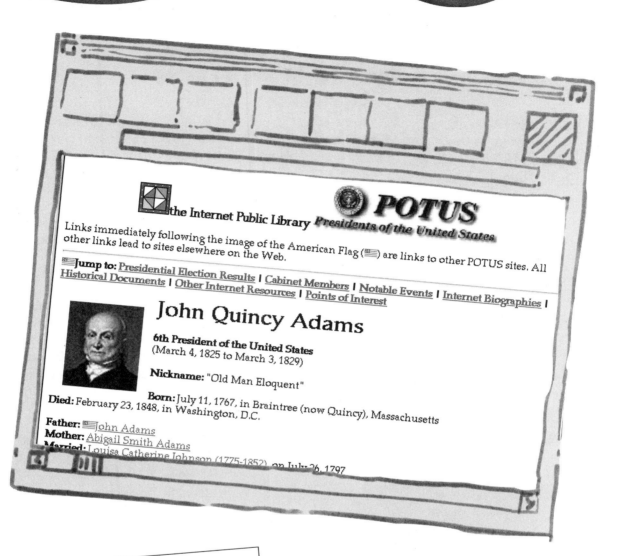

the Internet Public Library

POTUS *Presidents of the United States*

Links immediately following the image of the American Flag (🏴) are links to other POTUS sites. All other links lead to sites elsewhere on the Web.

🏴**Jump to:** <u>Presidential Election Results</u> | <u>Cabinet Members</u> | <u>Notable Events</u> | <u>Internet Biographies</u> | <u>Historical Documents</u> | <u>Other Internet Resources</u> | <u>Points of Interest</u>

John Quincy Adams

6th President of the United States
(March 4, 1825 to March 3, 1829)

Nickname: "Old Man Eloquent"

Born: July 11, 1767, in Braintree (now Quincy), Massachusetts

Died: February 23, 1848, in Washington, D.C.

Father: 🏴<u>John Adams</u>
Mother: <u>Abigail Smith Adams</u>
Married: Louisa Catherine Johnson (1775-1852), on July 26, 1797

Biography of a Statesman

http://www.ipl.org/ref/POTUS/jqadams.html

John Quincy Adams was the son of a President who himself became President. Learn about his life from his unusual childhood to his election as the sixth President of the United States by the vote of the House of Representatives, and find out why he became known as "Old Man Eloquent."

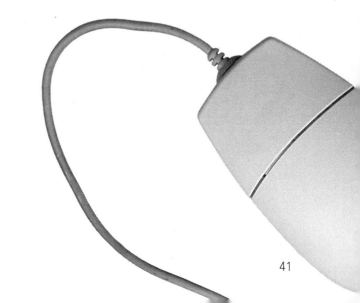

Seeing Is Believing

John Quincy Adams was the first President of the United States to be photographed. How times have changed! Today, the cameras click and whirl with—and without—Presidents' knowledge. Photography is a powerful medium that captures the times and moods of its subjects.

Objective

Students will use the medium of photography to capture a specific mood of a place or person.

Time Required

Two sessions of 1 1/2 hours each

Materials

- Digital camera or 35mm camera (disposable or standard)
- Film allowing for two pictures per student
- Mounting paper
- Glue sticks
- Pen
- Lined paper

Procedure

Show students a variety of photographs from magazines or private collections depicting places and people that create a specific mood. Ask students to discuss the mood of the photo and how this mood was achieved by the photographer.

Instruct students on the use of the camera and the limit on the number of pictures each student may take. In groups of four, students will be released to photograph scenes or persons that create a photographic "mood." Students should record the subject and the number of the film exposure for future identification.

Process digital photographs instantly and allow students to caption the photos, print and mount them on backing paper, and display them in the classroom gallery.

If lab processing is required, the groups will submit the film to you to have the film processed overnight. Returned prints will be captioned, mounted, and displayed.

Working on the Erie Canal

During the first year of John Quincy Adams's presidency, the Erie Canal was completed. A major inland waterway, it connected the city of New York, by way of the Hudson River, to the Great Lakes. By facilitating the transportation of people and products, the canal also eased the settlement of this region.

Objective
Students will create and illustrate a time line showing the construction of the Erie Canal and coinciding with world events.

Time Required
1 hour

Materials
• Reference books
• Internet access
• White shelf paper
• Pencils, colored pencils, and pens

Procedure
After reading the history of the Erie Canal, students in cooperative groups will design a time line of this period. They will use a variety of resources to determine what other world events were occurring simultaneously. These will be added to the time line, with the Erie Canal on top of the line and other events on the bottom. Be sure students seek events that represent world history, not simply Western Europe. Time lines will be illustrated and displayed for all to see.

Extensions
1. Students will research other prominent canals and the dramatic history connected to each.

2. John Quincy Adams was known to be an abolitionist who opposed ownership of slaves, but his prudent political side prohibited him from expressing these ideas publicly. If Adams were to write a letter to one of his closest friends expressing this conflict, how would the letter read?

3. Students will be able to distinguish the subtle and not-so-subtle differences between photographs from the early 1800s and those of today.

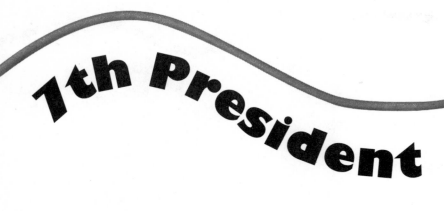

7th President

Andrew Jackson
1829 - 1837

Andrew Jackson, the first President from the frontier, gained national support when he defeated the British at New Orleans in the War of 1812. Known as "Old Hickory," Jackson retired to his home, the Hermitage, where he died in June 1845.

Alamo de Parras

http://www.flash.net/~alamo3/

The famous thirteen-day battle of the Alamo is chronicled in these pages, which tell the story of a small band of staunch defenders who were eventually overrun and killed by the forces of the Mexican general Santa Ana.

Indian Removal Act of 1830

http://www.alltel.net/~judymer/indexi.html

The Indian Removal Act of 1830 was an ill-conceived government operation that moved the Indian nations from Georgia further west, resulting in thousands of deaths. It eventually led to the reservation system, which broke the spirit of Native Americans.

THE HERMITAGE
Home of President Andrew Jackson

Jackson's Hermitage

http://hermitage.org/index.htm

Take a tour of the Andrew Jackson home, the Hermitage, which has been reconstructed to allow visitors to view the life and times of the nation's seventh president. Archaeological excavations continue today as we seek even more information about our leader's past.

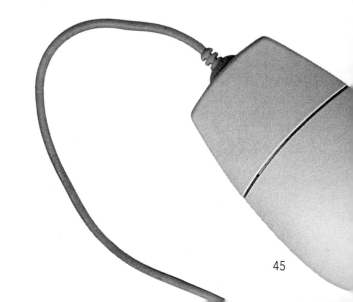

Point of View

During Jackson's first term of office, the Indian Removal Act of 1830 was passed. It allowed for the resettling of Indian tribes from the South to lands west of the Mississippi River. Jackson, known as an Indian fighter, used federal troops to force the Indian nations off their lands.

Objective
After reviewing the terms of the Indian Removal Act of 1830 and researching its effect on the Indian nations, students will play the roles of relocated tribespeople, expressing their feelings, fears, and viewpoints about the government's action.

Time Required
1 hour

Materials
- Copy of the Indian Removal Act of 1830
- Research materials
- Costumes based on traditional tribal clothing

Procedure
Assign students to research the history of the tribes relocated by the Indian Removal Act of 1830. These include the Cherokee, Seminole, Choctaw, Creek, and Chickasaw tribes. From the information gathered, students will understand the impact of relocation on these ancient nations and the ultimate destruction of their ways of life.

Dressed in costumes based on traditional clothing, each student will present a two-minute oral presentation. (Avoid any form of stereotyping in the costumes.) Each will play the role of an individual who has been relocated and tell how it affected his or her life. Roles should include all members of society: men, women, children, the young, the old, the weak, the strong, and the leaders.

Nicknames

Andrew Jackson is often referred to as "Old Hickory." It is said that he received this nickname as a result of a comment made by a fellow soldier, who stated that Jackson was as "tough as hickory."

Objective

Students will examine the nicknames of five Presidents and write a paragraph on the origin of each.

Time Required

45 minutes

Materials

• Internet access
• Reference books
• Writing materials

Procedure

In the history of the presidency, others have had nicknames that followed them through time. Ask students to make a list of five Presidents who also have had nicknames. They will then write a paragraph for each, giving a brief background on how the name came about and how each President reacted to his label.

Extensions

1. We often hear the phrase, "Remember the Alamo!" As an inquiry lesson, ask students "Why should we remember the Alamo?"

2. Find out the names of the members of Andrew Jackson's "Kitchen Cabinet," and discover why they were given this name.

3. Andrew Jackson's portrait appears on the twenty-dollar bill. Name the other Presidents whose faces are pictured on currency and coin.

8th President

Martin Van Buren
1837 – 1841

Martin Van Buren was the first Chief Executive born under the U. S. flag. It was an unfortunate twist of history that Van Buren inherited a cyclical economic depression that would wreak havoc during his term in office and across the nation for many years to come.

Lindenwald

http://www.regionnet.com/colberk/lindenwald.html

This site offers a unique look at the residence of the eighth President of the United States.

Welcome to the Martin Van Buren National Historic Site

http://www.nps.gov/mava/mvtoc000.htm

This site traces the politician's "magical" career with a time line of events and provides related links, including the Panic of 1837.

Martin Van Buren

Inaugural Address

Monday, March 4, 1833

The ailing President Jackson and his Vice President Van Buren rode together to the Capitol from the White House in a carriage made of timbers from the U.S.S. *Constitution*. Chief Justice Roger Taney administered the oath of office on the East Portico of the Capitol. For the first and only time, the election for Vice President had been decided by the Senate, as provided by the Constitution, when the electoral college could not select a winner. The new Vice President, Richard M. Johnson, took his oath in the Senate Chamber.

Fellow-Citizens: The practice of all my predecessors imposes on me an obligation I cheerfully fulfill—to accompany the first and solemn act of my public trust with an avowal of the principles that will guide me in performing it and an expression of my feelings on assuming a charge so responsible and vast. In imitating their example I tread in the footsteps of illustrious men,

Inaugural Address

http://www.cc.columbia.edu/acis/ bartleby/inaugural/pres25.html

Read the speech of this new President. The site visitor will determine whether his desires and dreams came to be, or whether they soon wilted in a time of trouble and economic despair.

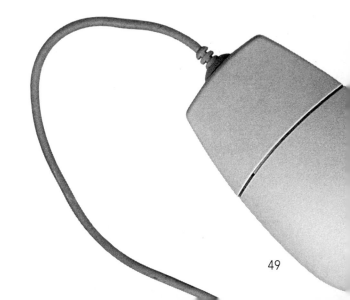

The Panic of 1837

Shortly after Martin Van Buren took office, the nation fell into its first major economic depression. The Panic of 1837 was sparked by a surplus of investments followed by the public's lack of confidence in the banking system. As hundreds of banks across the country failed and large numbers of people became unemployed, Van Buren saw it necessary to protect the federal funds. He called for the establishment of an independent treasury system, which Congress approved in 1840.

Objective

Students will be able to describe the events that occurred as the classroom reward system is drastically devaluated.

Time Required

4 days of activity
30 minutes of review and debriefing

Materials

• Classroom reinforcement point chart
• Prize chart
• Point tokens

Procedure

During the week, describe a new point system for good group behavior and completion of class projects. For each positive event, give students points that will be deposited in their group account (kept by you, the teacher). As the week goes on, give out huge numbers of point tokens while students tally the numbers for their group.

On the fourth day, inform the class that they have been assigned more points than the value of the prizes. Thus it will require many more points to actually purchase the prizes. The students must realize that the value of the points has decreased, since it will require more points to obtain any of the prizes. If students wait longer, the value of the points could increase or decrease. The students have to make a decision to take the points now or to take the chance of waiting until later. The teacher also informs the class that he or she has loaned about 25 percent of the points to another class, which will make it even more difficult for all the students to be given their points. Tell students who want the points to line up now.

At some point, you can stop the action and do a debriefing. Ask the students how they feel, what happened, and if they can see that this might have happened in the real world with the Panic of 1837. Continue the process feedback until the point is made. We suggest at this time that you break out gallon containers of ice cream and hot fudge and have fun!

1837

The Aroostook War, Not Really

The Aroostook War was actually a land or border dispute between lumbermen in New Brunswick and Maine. England and the United States had never agreed on an exact boundary in this region, and it became an issue in 1839. Van Buren sent General Winfield Scott to settle the dispute, which he did with a truce and the setting of the New Brunswick-Maine boundary.

Objective

Students will be able to establish specific boundaries using markers, maps, and collaborative planning.

Time Required

1 hour

Materials

- Maps of a designated area on the school site
- Measuring string marked every hundred feet
- Deed reproduction
- Butcher paper
- Pencils

Procedure

So that students can understand how important it is to mark and record the boundary of a designated site, a simulation will occur to facilitate this process. Give students a designated site (as described on a printout) no less than four hundred feet by five hundred feet. It may be much larger. Describe the site with identifiable landmarks such as fifty feet from the corner of Building Five and inclusive of the large elm tree to the west, etc. Each survey team of five students will have a different site, but they may overlap to provide some conflict. Students will mark their sites with markers (colored cones) and negotiate any conflict. The final product will be written deeds with property descriptions and a full map of all adjoining properties.

Extensions

1. Discuss why an independent treasury was introduced to hold and manage federal funds. Use examples of personal money management to make your point.

2. Van Buren was the first President to be born in the United States. He was of Dutch ancestry. Discover more about his Dutch ancestors by selecting aspects of his family's homeland for further study. Where is Holland? What does its current name, the Netherlands, mean? What are some general characteristics of the Dutch people in the 1800s and today?

3. What was the President's salary? What is the difference from the salary of today? What did President Van Buren decide to do with his earnings?

9th President

William H. Harrison
1841

Although his image prior to the election was one of a simple frontier Indian fighter who lived in a log cabin, William Henry Harrison was in actuality born into the Virginia aristocracy, studied the classics and history, and began studying medicine. He served in the army, later served as a governor, and became President in 1841. He was the first President to die in office.

William Henry Harrison

http://www.whitehouse.gov/WH/glimpse/presidents/html/wh9.htm

To be President of the United States is one of the greatest accomplishments a citizen could hope for. But for William Harrison, the journey to the White House ended in death from pneumonia after only one month in office. This site offers the biography of the first President to die in office.

Battlefield Museum/ Tippecanoe County Historical Association

http://jupiter.wvec.k12.in.us/battle/associat.html

This site provides an overview of the battle of Tippecanoe Creek. When Harrison was serving as governor, he led an army of soldiers against the village of Shawnee chief Tecumseh. He earned the name "Old Tippecanoe." It was not long before his 1840 campaign slogan rang out, "Tippecanoe and Tyler Too" in reference to the event and his chosen Vice-President, John Tyler.

William Henry Harrison

Inaugural Address

Thursday, March 4, 1841

President Harrison has the dual distinction among all the Presidents of giving the longest inaugural speech and of serving the shortest term of office. Known to the public as "Old Tippecanoe," the former general of the Indian campaigns delivered an hour-and-forty-five-minute speech in a snowstorm. The oath of office was administered on the East Portico of the Capitol by Chief Justice Roger Taney. The 68-year-old President stood outside for the entire proceeding, greeted crowds of well-wishers at the White House later that day, and attended several celebrations that evening. One month later he died of pneumonia.

Inaugural Address

http://www.cc.columbia.edu/acis/bartleby/inaugural/pres25.html

This site offers the longest inaugural address by the President serving the shortest amount of time in office. After his speech in a freezing snowstorm, Harrison remained outside the White House, greeting crowds of well-wishers and friends for several hours. Was it this action that one month later took his life?

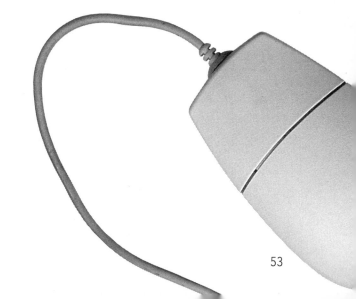

Who Takes the Place?

William Henry Harrison was the first President to die in office. He served only one month. As a result, Vice-President John Tyler became the tenth president.

Objective

Students will learn the law on secession to the presidency and identify the order of power. They will identify the men and women in today's government who could fill the position of President in the event of a catastrophe.

Time Required

45 minutes

Materials

- Almanac
- Copy of the law on succession to the presidency
- Internet access

Procedure

Instruct the students to read the law on succession to the presidency. This can be found in the almanac or online. List the order of succession:

President
Vice-President
Speaker of the House
President Pro Tempore of the Senate
Secretary of State
Secretary of Treasury
Secretary of Defense

Attorney General
Secretary of Interior
Secretary of Agriculture
Secretary of Commerce
Secretary of Labor
Secretary of Health and Human Services
Secretary of Housing and Urban Development
Secretary of Transportation
Secretary of Energy
Secretary of Education
Secretary of Veterans Affairs

Write down the names of the individuals who currently hold these offices. Discuss the kinds of political events or catastrophic disasters that would result in a low-ranking member taking office.

Medicine in the 1800s

President Harrison died of pneumonia in 1841. Would he have survived pneumonia if modern technologies and medicines were available?

Objective
Students will research, collect data, and chart the major causes of death in the 1800s.

Time Required
Two sessions of 1 hour each

Materials
- Internet access
- Almanac
- Encyclopedias
- Graph paper
- Pencils or pens

Procedure
Instruct students to research the accepted treatment of pneumonia by the medical profession in the nineteenth century. List other diseases that affected the death rate. Gather statistical information about each and chart the numbers on a graph.

Would the President have survived pneumonia if modern technologies and medicines were available? Go online to the many medical reference pages to discover today's treatments and medications.

Extensions
1. Research how President Gerald Ford was able to become President without ever being elected President or Vice-President.

2. In life, someone always is first at something. Usually we strive for that distinction. President Harrison had several firsts he probably would have preferred not to have. What were some of the firsts that President Harrison experienced?

3. During the 1840 campaign, Harrison focused his campaign on clever slogans rather than issues. Have your students find candidates in recent elections who may have done similar campaigning.

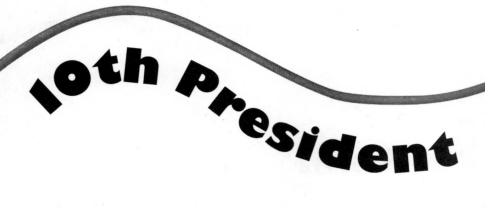

10th President

John Tyler
1841 - 1845

John Tyler offered new strength to the Presidency through his states' rights stance. However, this approach also provided greater division and separatism in the South.

Annexation of Texas

http://www.tsl.state.tx.us/lobby/annex/index.html

Learn more about how Texas became part of the United States. Following this annexation came two years of warfare between the United States and the Republic of Mexico.

Sherwood Forest, Home of President John Tyler

http://www.sherwoodforest.org/

Unlike the humble home of legendary hero Robin Hood, Sherwood Forest in England, John Tyler's home was the longest frame house in America on a site of 1,600 acres. You can visit this beautiful home as it was owned and preserved by the Tyler family.

the Internet Public Library

POTUS
Presidents of the United States

Links immediately following the image of the American Flag (▦) are links to other POTUS sites. All other links lead to sites elsewhere on the Web.

▦**Jump to:** Presidential Election Results I Cabinet Members I Notable Events I Internet Biographies I Historical Documents I Other Internet Resources I Points of Interest

John Tyler

10th President of the United States
(April 6, 1841 to March 3, 1845)

Nicknames: "Accidental President"; "His Accidency"

Born: March 29, 1790, in Greenway, Virginia
Died: January 18, 1862, in Richmond, Virginia

Father: John Tyler
Mother: Mary Marot Armistead Tyler
Married: Letitia Chrisitan (1790-1842), on March 29, 1813; Julia Gardiner (1820-1889), on June 26, 1844
Children: Mary Tyler (1815-48); Robert Tyler (1816-77); John Tyler (1819-96); Letitia Tyler (1821-1907); Elizabeth Tyler (1823-50); Anne Contesse Tyler (1825); Alice Tyler (1827-54); Tazewell Tyler (1830-74); David Gardiner Tyler (1846-1927); John Alexander Tyler (1848-83); Julia Gardiner Tyler (1849-71); Lachlan Tyler (1851-1902); Lyon

---

John Tyler

http://www.ipl.org/ref/POTUS/
jtyler.html

In a period marked by European immigration and the movement of pioneers westward on the Oregon Trail, John Taylor came to be President following the sudden death of President Harrison. This site is the biography of the man who was one of the first states' rights advocates.

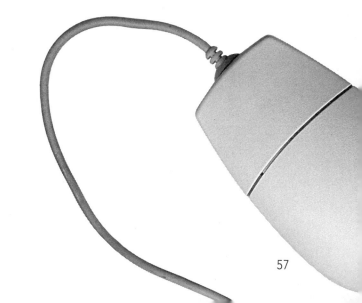

Lessons for Learning

Westward Ho

Beginning in the 1840s, thousands of pioneers headed west to the rich and fertile land of the Willamette Valley of Oregon. Many of the early immigrants who traveled the Oregon Trail packed only the items they could carry in their canvas-topped wagons as they traveled toward new lives in the West.

Objective

Following a discussion about the westward migration on the Oregon Trail, students will write a two-page story about the items they would pack if they were leaving their homes for a new place to live.

Time Required

1 hour

Materials

- Large shoe box
- Pencils or pens
- Lined writing paper

Procedure

Show students the empty shoe box. Inform them that they, like the early pioneers, will be leaving their homes and have limited space for the things they wish to carry. Each will make a list of the things to take on the journey. Remind students to make choices based on careful reasoning. They do not need to list pets, clothing, or food. Rather, have the students think about the personal items they deem important. Ask the students to think about the reasons for selecting an item. Is it sentimental or does it have a practical purpose? What items must be left behind because of space restrictions?

Following this brainstorming activity, students should write two-page papers about their choices, with supporting statements justifying their selections.

A Wave of Immigration

During the 1840s, the United States experienced a mighty wave of immigration from Europe. In the ten years following 1844, more than three million people came to the shores of this developing nation. Of those who sought a new start in a new land were 940,000 Germans and 1,300,000 Irish. Today immigration is still a dream for many who live in other lands. Many of today's immigrants arrive as part of an organized immigration system where applications for immigration are applied for and approved. In other cases, immigration is an illegal process, where thousands of people enter the country without proper approval or documents. Both groups seek immigration because of need.

Objective
Students will interview someone who immigrated to the United States.

Time required
45 minutes

Procedure
Have students interview someone who immigrated to the United States. Have them tell the story of the immigrant, offering the rationale and the process for immigration. Names of immigrants are not required. Many fascinating stories will be shared.

Extensions
1. Provide students the opportunity to travel the Oregon Trail using the CD-ROM program "The Oregon Trail III" by MECC. Students will experience a simulated trip on the trail, making choices and decisions along the way.

2. John Tyler was a strong advocate of states' rights. He sincerely believed that too much power at the federal level would threaten individual freedoms. This issue has continued to resurface over the next one hundred and fifty years. Have your students provide examples of why states' rights are important and what might happen if we didn't have the Tenth Amendment.

3. In 1844 a treaty with China opened up the Far East for U. S. trade. Have your students determine what would be the sought-after items for purchase and trade in this ancient land.

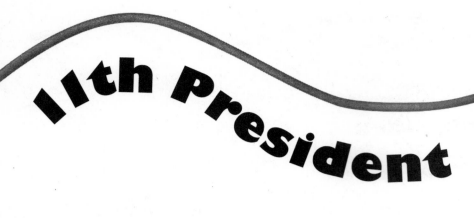

11th President

James K. Polk
1845 - 1849

James K. Polk expanded the borders of the nation to the Pacific Ocean. The victories over Mexico and resulting acquisitions brought California and New Mexico into the country but sparked bitter conflict between the North and South over slavery in the West.

James K. Polk

http://statelibrary.dcr.state.nc.us/
nc/bio/public/polk.htm

The first site for this eleventh President of the United States chronicles his life from a sickly child to his support of expansionism and the Manifest Destiny of the United States.

The Gold Rush in California

http://www.isu.edu/~trinmich/
fever.html

The California Gold Rush became the catalyst for President Polk to validate the extraordinary character of the expanding nation by encouraging westward movement. Easterners had their doubts about the abundance of western gold until President Polk corroborated early accounts of riches and discovery.

The U.S.-Mexican War, 1846-1848
A CONCISE HISTORY

Introduction
Countdown to War
The Northern Campaign
New Mexico Occupied
California Conquered
Scott's Invasion
The Peace Treaty
Appendices
Links to other sites

"After reiterated menaces, Mexico has passed the boundary of the United States, has invaded our territory and shed American blood upon the American Soil. She has proclaimed that hostilities have commenced, and that the two nations are at war."

- President James K. Polk, May 11, 1846

This website is "RECOMMENDED" by
ENCYCLOPEDIA BRITANNICA ONLINE

Read about the forthcoming
U.S.-Mexican War documentary
being produced by PBS affiliate
KERA-TV, Channel 13
in Dallas, Texas.

The U.S.-Mexican War

http://members.aol.com/dmwv2/mexwar.htm

Following the annexation of Texas, the United States and Mexico engaged in battle for two years. The war concluded with the signing of the Treaty of Guadalupe Hidalgo. Learn what this meant for the United States and Mexico.

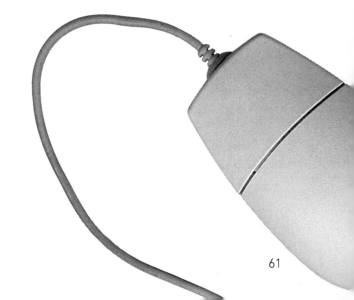

Discovering Gold

In the winter of 1848, gold was discovered in California. Although the news gradually spread east, few believed the reports until President James Polk validated the discovery in a statement made that December:

> "The accounts of the abundance of gold in that territory are of such extraordinary character as would scarcely command belief were they not corroborated by authentic reports of officers in the public service."

Newspapers carried the story, and the quest for gold in California began.

Objective
Students will participate in a simulated mining activity in which they will discover gold, weigh and measure their find, and determine its estimated value.

Time Required
1 1/2 hours

Materials
- Plaster of Paris
- Gold spray paint
- Small rocks
- Scales
- Hammers
- Safety glasses
- Notebook for recording
- Pencils or pens

Procedure
Prior to students' search for gold, spray-paint small rocks the color of gold. Let them dry overnight. Prepare a mixture of plaster of Paris. While still moist, mix in the gold rocks. Scoop out rounded handfuls of the plaster to form palm-sized balls. Prepare one ball per student. Set aside to dry. Find an area on the school grounds to hide the plaster rocks. Cover with bits of dirt, shrubbery, or sand.

Allow students to search for gold. Once they have found a plaster rock, carefully crack it open using a hammer. Be sure to wear safety glasses. Chip and pull away any excess plaster. Using a scale, weigh the gold rocks. Using a metric stick or ruler, measure the size of each nugget. Record the findings. Calculate the value of the find based on today's gold value. This information can be found online and is updated daily. Graph and chart the data.

The Department of the Interior

During James Polk's administration, the United States Department of the Interior was formed. Its role was to oversee the natural resources of the nation. There are a number of agencies within the department today. These include the Bureaus of Land Management, Fish and Wildlife Services, Indian Affairs, Land and Minerals, and Reclamation. The best-known agency is the National Park Service created in 1916.

Objective

The students will create a travel brochure for a national park.

Time Required

1 hour

Materials

- Internet access
- Encyclopedias
- Postcards and photographs
- Crayons, markers, or colored pencils
- Drawing paper
- Construction paper

Procedure

Students will select a national park and create a travel brochure. Access the Internet for the location, hours, and history of the various places. Download images, and print them using a color printer. E-mail the park for postcards and information that can be included in the students' brochures. Create a colorful threefold pamphlet.

If the technology is available, the same brochure can be created using a drawing program. Import images from the Internet (first check copyright restrictions) and type the text using word-processing software. Select from a variety of font styles and sizes to create a very professional piece of work. Print the final project using either a black-and-white or color printer.

Extensions

1. The Treaty of Guadalupe Hidalgo, which ended the Mexican War, was signed in February 1848. On a map of the United States, identify and label the area obtained by the United States as a result of the treaty.

2. We know much about the early days of the Gold Rush from the diaries and letters written by people who lived during this time of history. Read the letters of Dame Shirley (Mrs. Fayette Clappe) to understand a woman's view of the mining camps.

3. The first woman's rights convention was held in Seneca Falls, New York, in 1848. Women discussed such concerns as divorce, control of property, and voting. At woman's conferences held today, what are the topics and who attends the meetings?

12th President

Zachary Taylor
1849 – 1850

President Zachary Taylor was a career soldier who achieved the highest rank of Commander-in-Chief of the United States. Although President Taylor owned a cotton plantation in Mississippi, he was a nationalist and offered little support to the concept of slavery or Southern sectionalism. Because of his military career, he appealed to Northerners, while his ownership of nearly a hundred slaves won him Southern support.

Palo Alto Battlefield National Historic Site

http://www.nps.gov/paal/paal.htm

This battle, led by General Zachary Taylor, was the beginning of a two-year conflict between the United States and Mexico. Learn more about this turbulent time.

The Exhumation of President Taylor

http://www.ornl.gov/ORNLReview/rev27-12/text/ansside6.html

Doubting the reported cause of President Taylor's death, scholars convinced his descendants to exhume the body to see if he had actually died of arsenic poisoning. Discover what scientists learned in 1991, 141 years after his death.

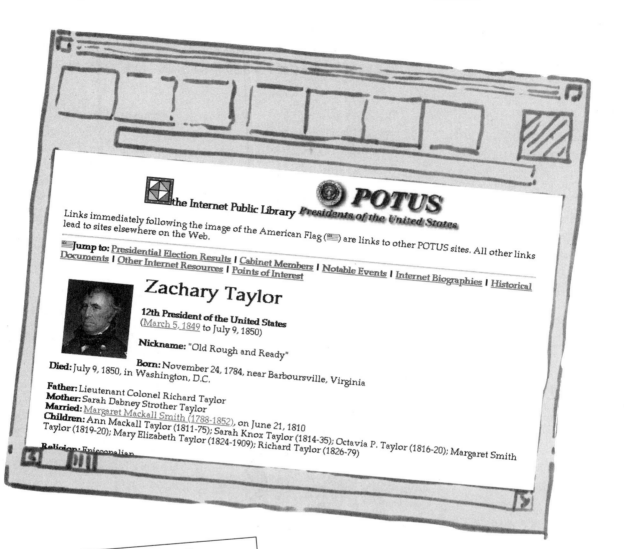

the Internet Public Library

POTUS
Presidents of the United States

Links immediately following the image of the American Flag (▥) are links to other POTUS sites. All other links lead to sites elsewhere on the Web.

▥**Jump to:** Presidential Election Results I Cabinet Members I Notable Events I Internet Biographies I Historical Documents I Other Internet Resources I Points of Interest

Zachary Taylor

12th President of the United States
(March 5, 1849 to July 9, 1850)

Nickname: "Old Rough and Ready"

Born: November 24, 1784, near Barboursville, Virginia
Died: July 9, 1850, in Washington, D.C.

Father: Lieutenant Colonel Richard Taylor
Mother: Sarah Dabney Strother Taylor
Married: Margaret Mackall Smith (1788-1852), on June 21, 1810
Children: Ann Mackall Taylor (1811-75); Sarah Knox Taylor (1814-35); Octavia P. Taylor (1816-20); Margaret Smith Taylor (1819-20); Mary Elizabeth Taylor (1824-1909); Richard Taylor (1826-79)

Religion: Episcopalian

Zachary Taylor

http://www.ipl.org/ref/POTUS/
ztaylor.html

Zachary Taylor never voted and never took an interest in politics before his run for the presidency when he was sixty-two years old. From his early days in Virginia as "Old Rough and Ready" in the Indian wars in Florida to his death in the White House, President Taylor was a colorful character of our expanding nation.

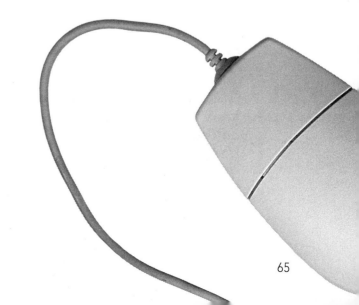

Lessons for Learning

Cinquains About Slavery

Zachary Taylor opposed the expansion of slavery into the new territories ceded by Mexico under the terms of the Treaty of Guadalupe Hidalgo. Controversy was brewing with the introduction of the Fugitive Slave Act. Slavery was a heated issue that would create division between the states.

Objective

Students will write a cinquain poem about slavery as it relates to the people, places, or events involved in slavery.

Time Required

45 minutes

Materials

- Research materials
- Writing materials

Procedure

Students will write a cinquain poem on the topic of slavery. They may choose any person, place, or event related to slavery and this era of history. Instruct students about the format of a cinquain poem. Specific rules apply to this form of poetry. As the poem begins to form, a specific shape can be seen:

Line 1: One two-syllable word that is the subject of the poem
Line 2: Four syllables describing the first line
Line 3: Six syllables showing action
Line 4: Eight syllables expressing an observation of the subject or describing a feeling
Line 5: Two syllables describing or renaming the subject

Examples:

Slavery
Human bondage
Despairing, suffering
Escaping to the Promised Land
Freedom

Have students share their poems with others in the form of a book. Using a word-processing program, print and publish the collection and bind into a classroom book.

Sing Along with the Forty-Niners

Following the discovery of gold in California, a steady flow of immigrants traveled west. The forty-niners, men and women who went to California in search of gold, used songs to tell of their plights and passions. These songs told of the expanding nation and the quest to move on.

Objective
Students will learn and sing songs of the Gold Rush that reflect the history and mood of the times.

Time Required
30 minutes

Materials
• CD player or cassette player
• Printed copies of the songs

Procedure
Teach the students the songs of the California Gold Rush. Visit the public library or local music store for a selection of titles. Sing along with the class, reviewing the history presented in each song. Introduce the following titles to the class:

"Sweet Betsy from Pike"
"Oh, My Darling Clementine"
"When I Went Out to Prospect"
"What Was Your Name in the States?"
"Joe Bower"

Extensions
1. Zachary Taylor was the first career soldier to attain the office of President. List the other Presidents with the same distinction. Report on their military achievements.

2. It was during Zachary Taylor's administration that overland mail service by wagon began between Independence, Missouri, and Santa Fe, New Mexico. The mail delivery required about thirty days from one end of the route to the other. Have your students calculate the distance on a map (or using a destination map locator on the Internet). Based on the number of days, figure out how far the wagon would travel in one day. If you can figure out the cost of mailing a letter in 1850, what was the cost per hundred miles? How does that compare to mail service and cost today?

3. What if the Panama Canal had been preceded by the Nicaragua Canal as a result of the Clayton-Bulwer Treaty signed by Britain and the United Stares? Locate Nicaragua on the map, and compare the probable location of a trans-canal with the established Panama Canal.

13th President

Millard Fillmore
1850 - 1853

Millard Fillmore exemplified that meager means, hard work, and basic competence could elevate a common man to the presidency. It was the "American Dream" come true. Fillmore is probably best remembered for his conciliatory policies that offered a postponement of the inevitable Civil War.

The Compromise of 1850

http://usd316.k12.ks.us/GPMS/1850.htm

The Compromise of 1850 admitted California into the Union as a free state, offered Utah and New Mexico the choice of accepting or rejecting slavery, and abolished slavery in the District of Columbia. Learn more about this national issue and how it affected an already unsettled Union.

Expansion of the Pacific—The Opening of Japan

http://www.smplanet.com/imperialism/letter.html

During this administration, the Far East represented a greater national interest. Commodore Perry visited Japan to establish relationships toward improved trade and commerce.

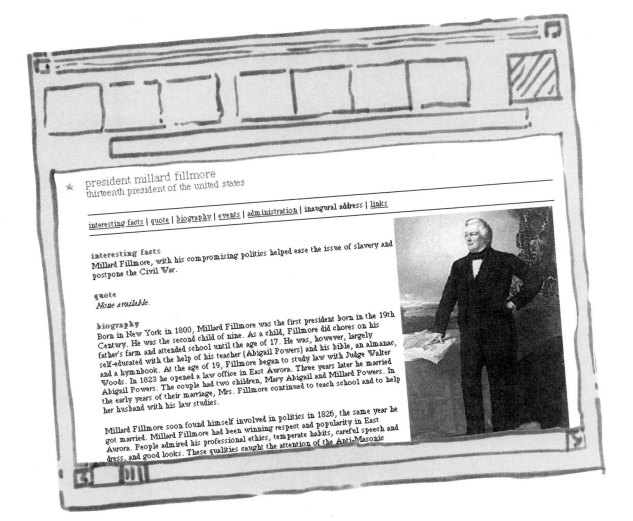

president millard fillmore
thirteenth president of the united states

interesting facts | quote | biography | events | administration | inaugural address | links

interesting facts
Millard Fillmore, with his compromising politics helped ease the issue of slavery and postpone the Civil War.

quote
None available.

biography
Born in New York in 1800, Millard Fillmore was the first president born in the 19th Century. He was the second child of nine. As a child, Fillmore did chores on his father's farm and attended school until the age of 17. He was, however, largely self-educated with the help of his teacher (Abigail Powers) and his bible, an almanac, and a hymnbook. At the age of 19, Fillmore began to study law with Judge Walter Woods. In 1823 he opened a law office in East Aurora. Three years later he married Abigail Powers. The couple had two children, Mary Abigail and Millard Powers. In the early years of their marriage, Mrs. Fillmore continued to teach school and to help her husband with his law studies.

Millard Fillmore soon found himself involved in politics in 1826, the same year he got married. Millard Fillmore had been winning respect and popularity in East Aurora. People admired his professional ethics, temperate habits, careful speech and dress, and good looks. These qualities caught the attention of the Anti-Masonic

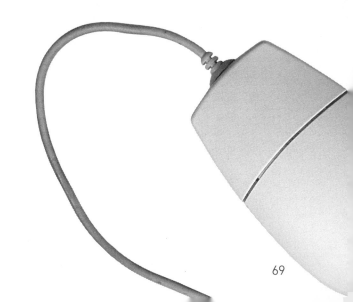

Millard Fillmore

http://library.advanced.org/12587/ contents/personalities/mfillmore/mf.html

This site is the home page for Millard Fillmore, thirteenth President of the United States. All pertinent data, including accomplishments and various events, are either described or linked. This site provides a good orientation to this early President.

Lessons for Learning

Japan Has Always Been There

With the admission of California to the Union, there was a much greater interest in Japan and the Far East for trade and commerce.

Objective

Students will be able to recognize the rich history of Japan. Students will participate in a culture day and will identify an artifact exemplifying the 1800s in Japan.

Time Required

2 hours
Cultural activities throughout the day

Materials

- Internet access
- Library resources
- Writing materials
- Materials specifically identified for the culture day

Procedure

Following an overview of geographical information related to Japan and the United States, students should research and develop a culture day related to Japan. Students in cooperative groups will develop centers, which they will share during the special day. Each center will have

a participative event and an artifact from Japan indicative of the 1800s. This should be a fun day with lots of artifacts,

interesting activities, events, some great food, Japanese music, and costumes.

The Compromise of 1850 Comes Home

As a part of the Compromise of 1850, California entered the Union as a free state. The other states won from conflicts with Mexico did not restrict slavery. Part of the compromise was that all fugitive slaves would be returned to their masters. It seemed rather inconsistent to forbid slavery in some states, to allow the choice in a few, and to allow slavery in others.

Objective
Students will debate issues related to the Compromise of 1850.

Time Required
45 minutes

Materials
• Charts
• Maps

Procedure
If you were in a state that was considered free, and if fugitive slaves were discovered, what would you do, and why? Assign roles and enter into a debate on the contrasting arguments. Reverse roles midstream to help students develop their debating skills.

Extensions

1. Why was it symbolic that California be a free state? How did this development shape California's future and culture?

2. The first cartoon depicting Uncle Sam as the symbol of the United States was published during the Fillmore administration. Have your students design and illustrate original cartoons of Uncle Sam.

3. Viewing the portraits and newspapers of the period, compare the dress of the 1850s with that of present times. Have dress and costume changed significantly? Is this true for the general population as well as for politicians?

14th President

Franklin Pierce
1853 - 1857

Franklin Pierce assumed that the nation was enjoying increasing domestic tranquility under his presidency. However, legislation such as the Kansas-Nebraska Act again magnified the slavery issue for the West, setting off new and increasingly sectional storms.

The Kansas-Nebraska Act

http://www.historyplace.com/lincoln/kansas.htm

This far-reaching Congressional Act allowed people in the territories to decide whether slavery would be permitted within their territorial boundaries. Find out what happened next.

The Life of Franklin Pierce by Nathaniel Hawthorne, 1852

http://www.tiac.net/users/eldred/nh/lfp.html

This view of the life and times of the fourteenth president was written by a contemporary. From his early life through the presidency, click and study along with early presidential scholars and those of today.

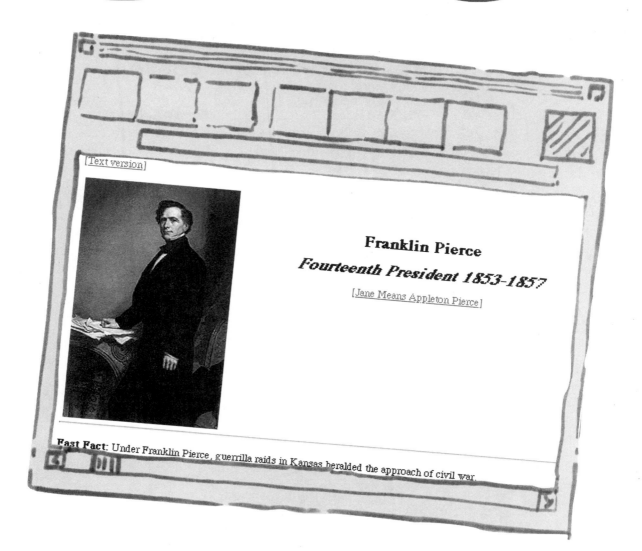

[Text version]

Franklin Pierce
Fourteenth President 1853–1857

[Jane Means Appleton Pierce]

Fast Fact: Under Franklin Pierce, guerrilla raids in Kansas heralded the approach of civil war.

Franklin Pierce

http://www.whitehouse.gov/WH/glimpse/presidents/html/fp14.html

Franklin Pierce became president during a time of apparent national tranquillity. Of course, the quiet was not to last for long. This site shows the unrest throughout the territories that would soon be the beginnings of a nation divided.

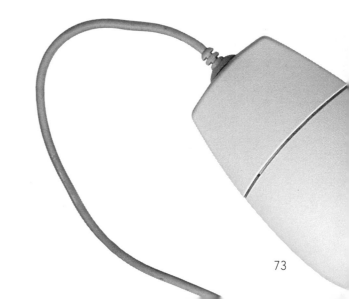

Lessons for Learning

The Gadsden Purchase

The Gadsden Purchase settled a longstanding border dispute between the United States and Mexico. The result provided a southern railroad route to the Pacific Ocean.

Time Required

1 hour

Materials

- Map
- Paints, crayons, markers, or colored pencils
- White butcher paper
- Reference materials

Objective

Students will be able to map the new southern railroad as it crossed the land obtained in the Gadsden Purchase from Mexico.

Procedure

Have your students learn about the route and the new states that it was to enter. Have them create a map of the new southern railroad with significant points of interest throughout the new states to the shores of the Pacific. Maps should be mounted, keyed, labeled, and displayed.

Campaign Slogans

Campaign slogans have been a part of political campaigns for many years. They are probably one of the most effective forms of advertising a candidate can have. Sometimes they are based on an event, rhyming words, the political climate, or the sign of the times. One such slogan that was used in the election campaign of Franklin Pierce was "We Polked you in 1844: we shall Pierce you in 1852."

Objective
Students will be able to identify past political slogans. Students will design and construct a political campaign poster with an appropriate slogan.

Time Required
Two sessions of 1 hour each

Materials
- Posterboard or piece of recycled cardboard
- Scissors
- Pencils
- Paints
- Internet access

Procedure
Review several slogans used in political campaigns from various periods in our history. Have students design their own slogans and campaign posters as a political language arts activity.

Extensions
1. Trace the route that Commodore Perry sailed on his historic mission to Japan in 1853. What were some of the hardships that his crew may have endured on this journey across the Pacific?

2. The Ostende Manifesto was a document that outlined a plan to buy Cuba from Spain. It was met with contempt by the southern European powers. Have the students learn more about Cuba and Spain. Where are the ties, and what might have happened if Cuba remained under Spanish control?

3. It is well known that Pierce installed the first central heating system in the White House. Prior to that time, how did the First Family keep warm during the chilly winter months?

15th President

James Buchanan
1857 - 1861

James Buchanan failed to see the sectionalism that was brewing in the heart of the nation in the late 1850s. His failure contributed to a worsening of conditions that brought the country to the brink of civil war.

The Dred Scott Decision

http://www.historyplace.com/lincoln/dred.htm

The History Place takes us to the time of the Supreme Court Dred Scott Decision, a case in which a slave sued for his freedom because he had been taken to a nonslave territory. Although Buchanan strongly disapproved of slavery, he felt powerless to limit slavery in the United States. This site provides evidence of the rising discontent between the North and the South.

The Pony Express Station

http://www.ccnet.com/~xptom/frm-history.html

"Riding with the ponies" might have been a slogan for the Pony Express. Inaugurated during the Buchanan administration, the Pony Express lasted for less than two years. However, it demonstrated the tenacity of those working to develop our young nation.

James Buchanan Foundation
James Buchanan

Home | Mansion | Harriet Lane | Gift Shop

James Buchanan

A Dedicated Public Servant

http://www.wheatland.org/buchanan.html

The fifteenth President of the United States served five terms in the House of Representatives, a decade in the Senate, as U. S. Minister to Russia, and later as Secretary of State under James Polk. This site chronicles his biography as a worthy servant of the government and the people.

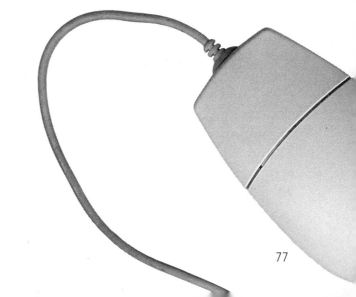

Dred Scott: A Classroom Trial

Just days after James Buchanan took office, the Supreme Court of the United States made its decision in the case of *Dred Scott* v. *Sandford*. Scott, a slave in Missouri, had sued for his freedom because he had been taken into a free territory. The court ruled that because Scott was a Negro and not considered by the Constitution to be a citizen of the United States, he had no rights to sue in federal court. Viewed by abolitionists as a pro-slavery stand, the decision further split an already divided nation.

Time Required
1 hour of preparation
1 hour of trial

Materials
• Internet access
• Library access
• Writing materials

Objective
Students will prepare and participate in the Dred Scott trial, weighing the rights of a slave who was suing for his freedom because he was taken to a state that prohibited slavery.

Procedure
Provide an overview of the historic context of slave states and free states. In addition, explore and explain Supreme Court decisions of the era. In this case, Dred Scott was suing for his freedom because he was taken to a free state. Your legal team must gather the evidence and prepare arguments for the Supreme Court that will influence the court either to allow Mr. Scott his freedom or force him to maintain his status as a slave. Monitor the preparations, and when it appears that both sides are ready to present the legal arguments, begin the trial.

Pony Express: A Long Ride for a Short Time

The Pony Express operated for less than two years, but the legend has lasted more than a hundred years.

Objective

Students will be able to describe the origin of the Pony Express, identify general routes, name characters of the period, and calculate miles and time for the delivery of a letter.

Time Required

Two sessions of 1 hour each

Materials

- Internet access (Wells Fargo Site, Pony Express)
- Library
- Pencils
- Paper
- Calculators
- Maps of the West

Procedure

Students will have ample opportunity to research the Pony Express. They might visit the Wells Fargo site on the World Wide Web. They should also seek out the main players and characters of this era (Mr. Wells, Mr. Fargo, Black Bart, Charley Parkhurst, etc.) and identify their roles.

Have students calculate the distance traveled between stations, speed at which riders traveled, time required, and number of horses and riders for the journey. Students can illustrate maps with keyed information to show what they have learned and how it relates to the Pony Express.

Extensions

1. Could Buchanan have prevented the Civil War? Historians disagree on his role. See what you can discover that might have changed the course of history and a nation.

2. A special romance was created by the Pony Express. After reviewing all the essential data related to this period, students will write short stories about being a part of the Pony Express experience.

3. Those who have had the courage to lead revolts seeking what they believe to be inalienable rights have often paid with their lives. Fortunately, their bravery has encouraged others to maintain the cause providing for lasting social change. John Brown, who was accused of leading a slave revolt, was seized at Harper's Ferry and hanged. Who are some other individuals in history who have paid either by death or long-term imprisonment for their courage in leading a social or political revolt?

16th President

Abraham Lincoln
1861 - 1865

Abraham Lincoln addressed a war-torn and divided nation in his second inaugural address: "With malice toward none, with charity for all, with firmness in the right as God gives us to see the right, let us strive on to finish the work we are in, to bind up the nation's wounds. . . ." Before he could finish this work, Lincoln was assassinated by an unemployed actor who had been born in the South.

So Many First Facts

http://www.ipl.org/ref/POTUS/
alincoln.html

We know about "Honest Abe," but not everyone knows the nickname "Illinois Rail Splitter." Lincoln was 6 feet 4 inches tall, the first President to wear a beard, and the first President to be assassinated. More interesting facts and links trace the life of one of the most famous Presidents.

The Gettysburg Address, November 19, 1863

http://lcweb.loc.gov/exhibits/gadd/

One of our nation's most famous speeches, the Gettysburg Address appears at this site along with the only known photograph of Lincoln at Gettysburg. Drafts of this speech are available for review.

The History Place™
presents

A. Lincoln: Lincoln's Photos and Words

http://www.historyplace.com/
lincoln/index.html

Travel through the past with this official time line and photo chronicle. All the major events of Lincoln's public life are listed in this comprehensive site. Fascinating photos provide a visual perspective.

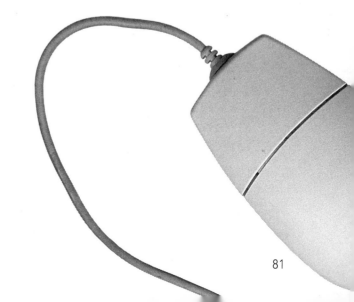

Lessons for Learning

Photographs of Lincoln

During Lincoln's administration, Mathew Brady made more than a third of the one hundred pictures taken of Lincoln.

Objective
Students will study the photographs of Lincoln and discuss the events that correspond to the dates of the images.

Time Required
1 1/2 hours

Materials
- Internet access
- Reference materials
- Portraits of Lincoln
- Bulletin board

Procedure
Instruct students to collect Brady's portraits of the President. Many can be found online or in references books. Date the photographs and create a time line of Lincoln's presidency. Mount the pictures on a bulletin board so that all the students can study the images. Look closely at the photographs, and note the changes in Lincoln's face as the Civil War progressed. Study the historical events that correspond to the dates, and discuss whether these events had an effect on the President. Draw conclusions based on the facts and the images.

Lincoln: A Multimedia Study of a President

Abraham Lincoln was a complex and fascinating man.

Objective

The students will create a multimedia presentation on the life and achievements of Abraham Lincoln.

Time Required

45 minutes to demonstrate the program

Several sessions to collect information and draft the presentation

1 hour per student at computer workstation

Materials

- Multimedia authoring program (e.g., HyperStudio)
- Computer
- Pencil
- Paper
- Construction paper
- Research materials

Procedure

Have students create a multimedia presentation focusing on Lincoln's life. Following their historical research, students will use one of the authoring programs available on the market today. Select a program that is simple to learn and easy to use. Know your needs; when purchasing a program, make sure it will run on your computer. Most software packages clearly state the amount of available RAM needed, the system require-

ments, and the type of computer. Instruct students on the use of the program. With so many students having computers at home, you may have an expert in your classroom without even knowing it.

Instruct the students about the features of a multimedia presentation: text, graphics, photographs, film clips, and sound. Demonstrate how to create links that enable the viewer to move through the presentation.

Prior to creating the digital version of the presentation on Lincoln, instruct students to draft their presentation on a large piece of paper. Edit and revise all text, making sure it is final, so that students can make the most of their time at the computer. While at the computer workstation, they can input the text, download images and movies, and create a unique look for the presentation. The complexity of the presentation is limited only by the student's creativity.

Extensions

1. Lincoln's sons were among the many children who lived in the White House. Have the students research the names of these children and other Presidents' children who lived there. Discover what became of them in adulthood, and how their childhood affected their lives.

2. Only 272 words long, Lincoln's Gettysburg Address is considered to be one of the finest speeches ever written. Visit the Library of Congress site to download the speech and study this famous work.

3. Although Mathew Brady photographed the President, he and his colleagues also documented the brutality and sorrow of the Civil War in the images captured on the battlefield. Have students research the use of photography and film in the wars that followed, such as World War I, World War II, the Korean War, the Vietnam War, and the Gulf War. They will discover that with each war, images were used to portray political attitudes of the times.

17th President

Andrew Johnson
1865 - 1869

With the sudden and tragic death of Abraham Lincoln, Andrew Johnson was the man of the moment. However, Johnson suffered many political defeats and conflicts and even faced impeachment.

War's Aftermath

http://odur.let.rug.nl/~usa/H/1990/ch5_p12.htm

Following the most horrific conflict in U. S. history, it fell upon Andrew Johnson to repair the Union. He had little success. This site offers a revealing view of the years immediately following the Civil War.

Impeachment and the Constitution

http://www.impeachment.org/frame_constitution_impeachment.htm

Although impeachment proceedings were brought against President Johnson, he was acquitted of the charges and served out his term. Enter the realm of the Constitution and discover the background, purpose, and procedures of impeachment.

1865 - 1869

Andrew Johnson

Eliza McCardle
Johnson

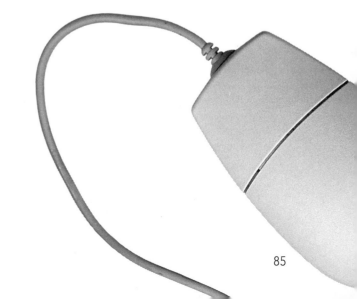

Andrew Johnson

http://www.peoples.net/~southbd/
pres16.html

Andrew Johnson assumed national leadership following the assassination of Abraham Lincoln. The only President to be impeached by the House of Representatives, Johnson was found not guilty and finished his term of office. This first site features the history and the man known as President Andrew Johnson.

Lessons for Learning

The Impeachment Process

When there is ample evidence that a sitting president has violated the law, the House of Representatives may formally move to impeach, indicating that a trial must be activated by the Senate. In the case of Andrew Johnson, the House of Representatives impeached him, sending the case to the Senate where, with a one-vote margin, he was found not guilty. If he had been found guilty, he would have been forced to leave office.

Objective

Students will be able to describe the impeachment process that almost removed Andrew Johnson from the presidency.

Time Required

1 hour

Materials

- Internet access
- Telephone
- Paper and pencils

Procedure

Students can determine the issues that brought Andrew Johnson to impeachment and the threshold of removal from office. Clarify the process of impeachment. Has any President ever been impeached and removed from office? Which President might have been impeached if he hadn't resigned?

Students can research the branches of government. How are the representatives in the House and the Senate elected, and on what basis? Find out the names of the representatives to the U. S. Senate and House of Representatives in your area and for the state in which you live.

Alaska, the Foolish Purchase

On March 30, 1867, the United States signed a treaty with Russia for the purchase of the territory of Alaska for the sum of $7 million. Was it a good investment? At the time, many said this purchase was foolish and a waste of good money. The land deal was labeled "Seward's Folly," after Secretary of State William H. Seward. People believed that the land was too far away, too far north from the continental United States, and too frigid most of the year to have any practical use. Of course, Alaska has become an extraordinary valuable asset in terms of natural resources and tourism, but it is still cold!

Objective
Students will research the purchase of Alaska. Students will compare the amount of money spent for the land to the purchasing power it has in today's economy.

Time Required
Two sessions of 1 hour each

Materials
• Library resources
• Internet access
• Calculators
• Chart paper
• Writing materials

Procedure
Have students learn more about Alaska as it was in the 1800s and as it is today. Why did Russia possess it, and why did they want to sell it? Did they make a mistake selling it to the United States? What valuable natural resources were discovered there, and what far-thinking technological scheme was used to exploit these? What other living natural resources flourish in Alaska? Why is Alaska still considered the last frontier?

Make a chart comparing the entire state of Alaska, purchased for $7 million to purchases that cost $7 million today. What is the salary of a professional basketball player? The cost to build one school? The cost to build one mile of a new four-lane expressway?

Extensions
1. During the Reconstruction Era, new government positions in the Southern states were established and filled by people called "carpetbaggers" and "scalawags." Who were these individuals, and what problems were caused by their presence? Where did these colorful names originate?

2. The Thirteenth Amendment abolished slavery. Have students play the roles of a group of former slaves discussing what the future might hold. What would the conversation of slave owners be like?

3. Why was the ratification of the Fourteenth Amendment so important? Students can dramatize their arguments.

IS IT WORTH THE PRICE?

18th President

Ulysses S. Grant
1869 – 1877

Ulysses S. Grant was one of the great symbols of the Union victory over the South in the Civil War. As a renowned general with the Union forces, he was a natural for the Republican nomination and ascendancy to the presidency.

Ulysses S. Grant

http://www.ipl.org/ref/POTUS/
usgrant.html

This site offers a good array of general information about Ulysses Simpson Grant. From his religious affiliation and the election results of 1868 and 1872 to a myriad of biographical and historical links, there is more about Ulysses Grant than simply, "Who is buried in Grant's tomb?"

Ulysses S. Grant Network Home Page

http://saints.css.edu/mkelsey/
gppg.html

Click on the links to find a useful guide for students, a five-part life history, stamps, a chronology, and much more.

Ulysses S. Grant Home Page

http://www.mscomm.com/~ulysses/

This Ulysses S. Grant home page asks and answers the many questions related to the incomparable military general and the eighteenth President of the United States. Explore the voluminous text and many rare photos.

How Did They Make It Meet?

In 1869 the first transcontinental railroad was completed with the joining of the western segment and the eastern segment at Promontory Point, Utah.

Objective
Students will be able to identify the significant issues related to the completion of the transcontinental railroad.

Time Required
2 hours

Materials
- Internet access
- Library resources
- Writing materials

Procedure
Why was the Golden Spike significant? What effect did the railroad have on the country? And how did they get the two separate tracks to meet perfectly at Promontory Point? Students can indulge in a research project on one or more of these topics. They can dramatize the pounding of the Golden Spike and give speeches that may have been made on that spot. Students can also illustrate this very important event in American history. Display and share their work.

The Fifteenth Amendment: What Did It Really Mean?

The Fifteenth Amendment to the Constitution provided voting rights to citizens regardless of race. With the passage of the Fifteenth Amendment came the realization that voting rights were still not universal in America.

Objective
Students will be able to identify and dramatize the conditions and ramifications of the Fifteenth Amendment.

Time Required
Two sessions of 1 hour each

Materials
• Research materials
• Library resources
• Internet access
• Writing materials

Procedure
Have students provide their reaction to this change in our nation's governance. Create a simulation where participants reenact the feelings on election day for those constituent groups who could still not exercise their right to vote, or who had been overlooked by this amendment.

Extensions
1. Ulysses S. Grant signed the act that created Yellowstone National Park. What significance did this hold? Why was it deemed necessary to protect this natural resource? Access Yellowstone National Park on the World Wide Web and visit this true wonder of the world.

2. Barbed wire was first made in 1873. It brought an end to the open range of the West. What significance, both positive and negative, did this innovation have in our history? Students could write a journal entry from the point of view of a small farmer and from that of a cattle rancher.

3. The National Woman's Suffrage Association was founded in 1869 by Susan B. Anthony and Elizabeth Cady Stanton. What was the focus of their work? How many years did the struggle continue until all women had equal voting rights?

19th President

Rutherford B. Hayes
1877 - 1881

Rutherford B. Hayes pledged protection of the rights of black Americans in the southern states, but he simultaneously promoted the restoration of local self-government. With this pledge came the withdrawal of post-Civil-War troops, which permitted the "solid South" to be reborn.

Inaugural Address

http://www.columbia.edu/acis/
bartleby/inaugural/pres35.html

After a disputed election, Rutherford B. Hayes assumed the presidency with this inaugural address on Monday, March 5, 1877.

Rutherford B. Hayes

http://www2.whitehouse.gov/WH/
glimpse/presidents/html/rh19.html

This site reveals, along with other interesting biographical facts, that Hayes was the first President to use a telephone installed in the White House.

Rutherford B. Hayes Presidential Center

http://www.rbhayes.org/default.htm

This is truly a presidential home page. The site takes you to the home of President Hayes as well as to the first library dedicated to the papers of a U. S. President.

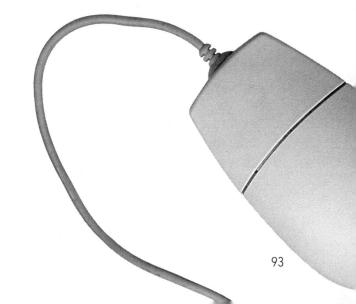

Chinese Immigrants and the Development of America

No sooner had Reconstruction ended in the South than new monetary and labor problems surfaced in both the East and the West. In the East and Midwest, striking railroad workers fought battles with state militia. Hayes sent in federal troops to attempt to calm the dispute. In the West, another labor dispute involved Chinese immigrants. A treaty between China and the United States had allowed unlimited immigration rights. In 1880 a new treaty was signed, giving the United Sates the right to totally regulate, limit, or suspend immigration from the Far East. Chinese immigration offered a diverse cultural richness to America.

Objective
Students will research the Chinese culture in America, culminating their study with a Chinese Cultural Awareness Day.

Time Required
2 weeks of social studies, culminating with a half day of cultural activities

Materials
• Internet access
• Library resources
• Guests
• Materials for Cultural Awareness Day

Procedure
What did the Chinese bring to this new land, and what was in store for them upon arrival? What role did they play in the development of the West? Have students research the Chinese in America and the cultural influence that exists today. Students can organize a Chinese Cultural Awareness Day reflecting the period of the 1880s. This should be complete with food, music, literature, art, guests, and traditions.

Phone Home . . . to the White House

President Hayes was the first President to have a phone installed in the White House. This was quite an innovation, but it certainly required other phones to be installed in and around Washington to become effective. From that time on, the phone has been the staple of communication between all branches of government as well as a vehicle to express views and concerns. Many years later when Jimmy Carter was in the White House, he promoted a "Phone the President Day." As more than nine million people tried to call the White House simultaneously, all phone lines in and around Washington were temporarily gridlocked.

Objective
Students will learn about telephone access to the White House in the 1800s and today.

Time Required
Several sessions of 1 hour each

Materials
• Phone books
• Directory assistance online
• Internet access
• Chart paper
• Writing materials

Procedure
Public officials in many capacities are available via telephone. Develop a phone chart of government officials you could call. Try to find 800 numbers for officials who are out of your telephone area. Try to find people you would like to interview. Groups of four students can make arrangements (with your assistance) to place a conference call and interview the official. Following the call, send a thank-you note or e-mail message.

Extensions
1. Colorado became the thirty-eighth State of the Union. Partake in an Internet journey through Colorado. Don't forget the majestic Rocky Mountains.

2. Hayes was a champion speller in elementary school and placed a high value on spelling and writing. What were some of the words that had special significance during the Hayes presidency? Conduct a spelling bee using these and other words related to the government.

3. Lucy Webb Hayes was the first wife of a President to have a college degree. She was also known as "Lemonade Lucy" because she served guests lemonade instead of alcoholic beverages. What is significant about these two facts at this time in history?

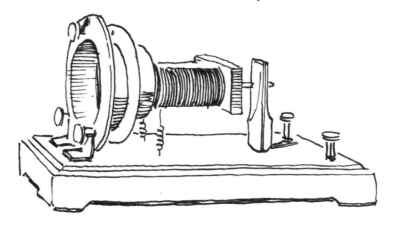

20th President

James A. Garfield
1881

James Garfield was the last President to have been born in a log cabin. Garfield attempted to fight corruption and to bring presidential prestige back to the White House, but his life was cut short when an assassin shot him at a Washington railroad station. He died during the same year he took office.

James A. Garfield

http://www.grolier.com/presidents/ea/bios/20pgarf.html

As a result of an assassin's bullet, James A. Garfield had a very short tenure as President of the United States. A biography of his early life, military service, and public service career, as well as his presidency, is chronicled on this site.

Alexander Graham Bell and the Garfield Assassination

http://www.historybuff.com/library/refgarfield.html

Learn about the coil-spring bed and the elusive bullet. This site tells the story of how Alexander Graham Bell invented a honing device that might have saved the President's life by making it possible to find the exact location of the bullet lodged in the President's chest. Discover what happened and why.

James A. Garfield

Lucretia Rudolph
Garfield

James Garfield— Quick Facts

http://www.peoples.net/~southbd/ pres19.html

This site, which is emblazoned with the thirty-eight-star flag, provides the young historian with additional interesting facts about the twentieth President.

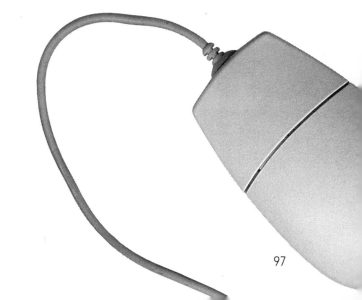

Lessons for Learning

The Bullet

Following the shooting of President Garfield at a train station, doctors were unable to locate the bullet lodged in his chest. Newspapers began to carry the story, and eventually Simon Newcomb of Baltimore was interviewed. He had been experimenting with electricity and wire coils, but had not perfected the device. Although the coil could be placed near metal and produce a faint hum, the hum was almost impossible to hear. Through the combined efforts of Newcomb's innovation and of Alexander Bell's invention of the telephone, there appeared to be some hope for the dying President.

Objective

Students will research how the invention of the telephone almost saved President Garfield's life.

Time Required

45 minutes

Materials

• Internet access
• Traditional resources

Procedure

As an inquiry lesson, students can discover how Alexander Bell and the invention of the telephone became involved in the attempt to locate the bullet in the President. Discover the simple reason why it did not work.

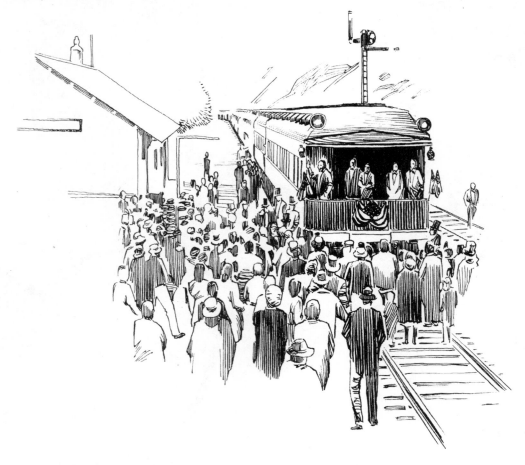

The Assassins

In the history of the country, there have been a number of assassinations of and assassination attempts on the Presidents. Individuals who perpetrated these acts had personal or political reasons.

Objective
Students will investigate assassination attempts on the Presidents and determine which events could have been changed to prevent tragedies from taking place.

Time Required
45 minutes

Materials
• Internet access
• Traditional resources
• Writing materials

Procedure
Instruct students to research the following Presidents and assassins:

Abraham Lincoln, assassinated by John Wilkes Booth

James Garfield, assassinated by Charles Guiteau

William McKinley, assassinated by Leon F. Czolgoz

John F. Kennedy, assassinated by Lee Harvey Oswald

Gerald Ford, assassination attempts by Lynette Alice "Squeaky" Fromme and Sara Jane Moore

Harry S. Truman, assassination attempt by Oscar Collazo and Griselio Torresola

Ronald Reagan, assassination attempt by John W. Hinckley, Jr.

Following a discussion of the circumstances that surrounded these events, ask students to think about how history could have been different if the people, places, or times had somehow been altered.

Extensions
1. James Garfield was the last President born in a log cabin. Create log cabins using a variety of materials, such as pretzels, tongue depressors, cinnamon sticks, graham crackers, or clay. List the names of other Presidents born in log cabins.

2. President Garfield eventually died from complications caused by the bullet remaining in his body. Interview a community doctor to find out how the medical profession today treats similar types of wounds, and how they prevent infection.

3. Prior to becoming President, Garfield had been a professor and college president, as well as Civil War general and a Congressman. Several past Presidents have worked as educators. Why do you think this profession could be useful for a future President?

GENERAL
COLLEGE PRESIDENT
PROFESSOR
CONGRESSMAN

21st President

Chester A. Arthur
1881 - 1885

The presidency of Chester Arthur can perhaps be summed up with the quote from publisher Alexander K. McClure: "No man ever entered the Presidency so profoundly and widely distrusted, and no one ever retired . . . more respected."

More Facts

http://www.ipl.org/ref/POTUS/caarthur.html

Packed full of historical information and related links, this site offers insight into the life and presidential term of Chester A. Arthur.

The History Behind the Man

http://www2.whitehouse.gov/WH/glimpse/presidents/html/ca21.html

"Gentleman Boss" and "Elegant Arthur" are the nicknames bestowed upon President Arthur. This general site provides biographical information and the important links for understanding the "man who never ran for President."

CHESTER A. ARTHUR

21st President (1881–1885)

No higher or more assuring proof could exist of the strength and permanence of popular government than the fact that though the chosen of the people be struck down, his constitutional successor is peacefully installed without shock or strain . . . "
— Inaugural address, 1881

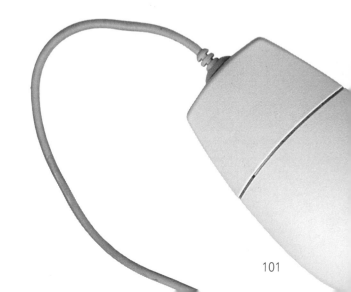

Chester A. Arthur

http://www.clark.net/silhan/pres1.htm

This site contains a formal biography of the twenty-first President of the United States. The visitor to this site will be whisked through time to related topics of study.

My Life Belongs to the People

President Arthur was quoted as saying, "I may be President of the United States but my private life is my own damn business." In actuality, for a person who is the people's representative, personal life and public life become one.

Objective
Students will be able to discuss the needs of public figures to maintain some privacy versus the desire of the people to discover what they can.

Time Required
Two sessions of 1 hour each

Materials
- Internet access
- Library resources
- Newspapers
- Magazines
- News broadcasts
- Writing materials

Procedure
Can a President maintain a private life away from the eyes of the public? Should the public, through the news media, respect the desires of the President and

the First Family, or does the public have the right to know at any price? Explore newspaper articles, photographs, magazines, and news broadcasts for several modern Presidents, and determine the appropriate behavior of the public and the press. Have students present their findings to the class, providing visual examples to support their position.

Who Owns the President's Personal Papers?

It is customary for historians to review the personal papers of a President to learn more about the man, the events, and the times. These voluminous caches of paper, digital information, film, and audio recordings have been archived in presidential libraries and national archives. President Arthur chose to ignore this tradition and burned all of his personal papers, thus creating a void for future study of his life and times.

Objective
Students will be able to describe the characteristics of presidential papers and the role they play in providing a record of history.

Time Required
Two sessions of 45 minutes each

Materials
• Internet access
• Research and writing materials
• E-mail

Procedure
In this lesson, explore—via the Internet and through interviews—the availability of presidential papers for public and scholarly study. In addition to the above-named sources, students might choose to e-mail a history professor at a local university.

They should formulate questions that can provide greater insight into the importance of these primary sources.

Extensions
1. Two major innovations in construction occurred during Arthur's presidency. The Brooklyn Bridge, at that time the world's longest suspension bridge, and the Home Insurance Building, the first metal frame skyscraper, were constructed. Students can research either of these two engineering marvels and, with appropriate materials, construct a model of their own.

2. The four standard time zones replaced nearly a hundred different "railroad" times. Students can be given problems determining arrival, departure, and travel time moving from one time zone to another.

3. Two forms of large-crowd entertainment became popular in this period. Buffalo Bill's Wild West Show toured the United States and Europe, and the Metropolitan Opera House opened in New York City. Students can reenact some of the events from the Wild West Show and be exposed to the life and magic of the opera.

22nd & 24th President

Grover Cleveland
1885 – 1889
1893 – 1897

Grover Cleveland, who served as the twenty-second and twenty-fourth President, was the only Commander-in-Chief to leave the White House and be elected for a second term four years later. His terms were characterized by strife and conflict: he tried to discourage special-interest groups from influencing the presidency, he angered the railroads, and he had to deal with an economic depression.

Glover Cleveland

http://www.ipl.org/ref/POTUS/gcleveland.html

Grover Cleveland is profiled on this Internet Public Library site. Although this is a general information site, the links provide interest and motivation related to the study of this President. Read Cleveland's obituary or listen to an audio of the campaign between Cleveland and Benjamin Harrison.

Statue of Liberty

http://lcweb2.loc.gov/ammem/today/

Visit the Statue of Liberty site to find facts, news, and information. This gift from France has come to symbolize our nation. President Cleveland dedicated the statue on October 28, 1886. The Statue of Liberty stands as a beacon to all who seek refuge upon our shores.

Glover Cleveland Home Page

http://www.rain.org/~turnpike/
grover/TopPage.html

Learn about Grover Cleveland's childhood and political career. Links guide you to additional bibliographical sites, inaugural addresses, and much more.

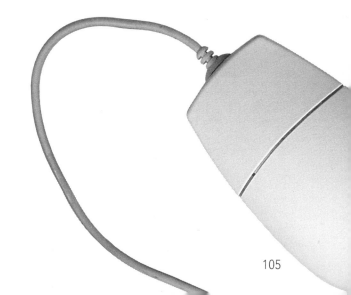

Lessons for Learning

Election

In order to be elected President of the United States, candidates must campaign to get their messages and platforms out to the public.

Objective
Students will organize an election.

Time Required
Three sessions of 1 hour each

Materials
- Posterboard
- Construction paper
- Markers, pens, colored pencils
- Sample campaign and voting materials
- Tape
- Large cardboard box to hold ballots

Procedure
Students will design their own classroom election. Select two or three students to play the role of the presidential candidates. These individuals should demonstrate the qualities of responsibility and leadership. They will be responsible for writing and delivering a campaign speech. Select campaign managers who will oversee the distribution of political materials. Assign the following tasks to the remaining students:

- Writing mottoes and slogans for the candidates
- Making and distributing campaign posters and buttons
- Designing and printing voting ballots
- Building an election booth and ballot box
- Creating a one-minute commercial using a video camera or multimedia computer program
- Writing editorials about the candidates for the classroom newspaper

Select a Tuesday morning for the student candidates to campaign and deliver their speeches. Following the activity, have each member of the class cast a secret vote. Count the ballots and announce the winner.

A Symbol

The Statue of Liberty, given to the United States in 1886 by France, has become a symbol of the United States. Millions of immigrants have passed this statue and have dreamed of freedom and opportunity.

Objective
Students will design a monument that could be built to welcome immigrants from the Pacific.

Time Requirement
45 minutes

Materials
- Internet access
- Traditional resources
- Pencils, pens, markers, colored pencils
- Drawing paper

Procedure
Using the Internet and traditional resources, students will discover the history behind the Statue of Liberty. Study the design created by sculptor Frederic Auguste Bartholdi and engineer Alexandre Gustave Eiffel. Trace the history of immigration into the United States to discover why the statue has become a symbol of freedom.

Instruct students to design a new monument that could be placed on the Pacific coast. Sketch the design on a large piece of drawing paper. Ask students to think about the following questions when designing their statue:

- What would the statue look like?
- Where would the statue be located?
- Why would this location be selected?
- What materials would be used to build the statue?
- What could the statue represent?
- What name would be given to the statue?

Each student will give a short oral presentation showing the new design and explaining the selection.

Extensions
1. Grover Cleveland has been described as a man respected for his "courage, honesty and patriotism." What does this mean?

2. Research the connection between a popular candy bar and President Cleveland.

3. Grover Cleveland has the distinction of being the only president to be reelected after being voted out of office. What did he do during the four years between his two terms? Find out the roles Presidents play after they leave office.

23rd President

Benjamin Harrison
1889 - 1893

Benjamin Harrison was one of the first to conduct a "front-porch" campaign for the presidency, delivering short speeches to the various delegations that would visit him in Indianapolis. In the election of 1888, he received 100,000 fewer popular votes than his opponent but captured the electoral college.

Benjamin Harrison

http://www.whitehouse.gov/WH/glimpse/presidents/html/bh23.html

Although the twenty-third President, "Little Ben," was only 5 feet 6 inches tall, he was big enough to follow the footsteps of his grandfather, William H. Harrison, the ninth President. View images and links related to his life and presidency. Discover the important pieces of legislation he signed dealing mainly with trusts, monopolies, and tariffs.

The President Benjamin Harrison Home

http://www.surf-ici.com/harrison/

Visit the home of Benjamin Harrison in Indianapolis, Indiana. Take a tour of this beautiful home, and visit the exhibits that reflect an era of history.

Wounded Knee Home Page

http://www.dickshovel.com/WKmasscre.html

The Wounded Knee home page sheds light on the historic event that might have been the final, fatal blow for a group of Native Americans.

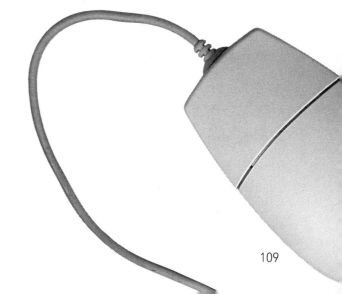

Lessons for Learning

Old Glory

Benjamin Harrison ordered that the U. S. flag fly over the White House and other government buildings.

Objective
Students will make replicas of the flags of the United States and list the Presidents who served at the time of each.

Time Required
1 hour

Materials
- Red, white, and blue construction paper
- Internet access
- Reference materials

Procedure
Trace the history of the flag, and note the changes. Collect samples of each design from the Internet and traditional resources. Using red, white, and blue construction paper, students will make the flags of the United States. Assign a different style of flag to each student. Distribute a piece of white construction paper to each student. Cut out the red strips, the white stars, and the blue background from construction paper. Position and glue. When the flags are dry, hang them on a large bulletin board. Below each, post a list of the Presidents who served during the times these flags flew.

Ellis Island

Twelve million immigrants from Eastern and Central Europe came through Ellis Island between 1895 and 1924. In 1892 the federal government opened a processing station to handle the massive numbers making their way into the United States. Many were unfamiliar with the language and culture of this new country.

Objective
Students will participate in an exercise simulating immigration through Ellis Island.

Time Required
30 minutes

Materials
• Word-processing software with pictograph or hieroglyphic font
• Pencils or pens

Procedure
Before students enter the classroom, type the following questions using a word-processing program. Add any additional questions that may apply to your class or curriculum.
• What is your name?
• What is the name of the city in which you live?
• When is your birthday?
• How many people are in your family?
• What items are you carrying?
• Whom do you live with?

When the questionnaire is completed, select a pictograph or hieroglyphic font from your word-processing program and format the text. Print a copy for each student, and place it facedown on each desk. It might look like the following:

✳✳☀▼ ✳▲ ▯□◆▯ ■☀○✳✝
✳✳☀▼ ✳▲ ▼✳✳ ■☀○✳ ▯✳
▼✳✳ ✳✳▼▮ ✳■ ▶✳✳✳✳ ▯□◆
●✳◆✳✝
✳✳✳■ ✳▲ ▯□◆▯ ○✳□▼✳✎
✳●▯†
★▯▮ ○☀■▮ ▯✳□□●✳ ☀▯✳
✳■ ▯□◆▯ ☀☀○✳●▯†
✳✳☀▼ ✳▼✳○▲ ☀▯✳ ▯□◆
✳☀□□▮✳■✳†
✳✳▯ ✳▯ ▯□◆ ●✳◆✳ ▶✳▼✳†

When students enter the classroom, motion them to take their seats. Smile cordially and model for them to turn their papers over and begin answering the questions. Do not speak to them, only motion. Allow ten minutes to complete the form.

Following the activity, conduct a classroom discussion, asking the students to express what they felt as the process was taking place. Compare it to what the immigrants in the 1890s may have felt. Draw conclusions.

Extensions
1. During the Harrison administration, a menagerie of animals, including a pet goat, roamed the grounds of the White House. Discover the types of pets each President has owned while in office, and make a chart showing the information collected.

2. The battle of Wounded Knee on the plains of South Dakota was the last major battlefield conflict between Native Americans and U. S. Army troops. It resulted in the massacre of nearly 200 Indians. At this point in history, Native Americans experienced total hopelessness. After reading aloud some of the written accounts of this battle and the many broken treaties, have them write journal entries from the perspective of the tribal elders.

3. This was the era of the temperance movement, which was led by crusader Carry A. Nation. It was becoming increasingly clear that alcohol abuse led to the abuse of women and children, absenteeism from work, and public fighting. Discuss these issues with your students, and point out the similarities of behavior in our society today. Use examples of spousal abuse, child abuse, drunk driving, and public fighting. Be sure to inform students of local resources that may offer assistance to those in need.

25th President

William McKinley
1897 - 1901

William McKinley was elected as the "agent of prosperity" by his supporters to bring the nation out of the economic depression of the 1890s. However, international relations dominated McKinley's presidency during his first and second terms, until his tragic assassination at the Buffalo Pan American Exposition in 1901.

William McKinley

http://www.ipl.org/ref/POTUS/wmckinley.html

Facts and figures related to the twenty-fifth President of the United States fill this site. From his nickname, "the Idol of Ohio," to presidential election results, research the many accomplishments of this national leader.

William McKinley Early Motion Pictures—From the American Memory Historical Collections

http://lcweb2.loc.gov/

See movies of McKinley's funeral and a panoramic view of his home. Other early movies are featured in this site. To access the collection, type "McKinley" in the search box.

The Era of William McKinley

These pages provide information about the presidency of William McKinley.

- The Ohio Historical Society, the Society for the History of the Gilded Age and Progressive Era, and the Department of History of The Ohio State Univesity are sponsoring a **Conference on the Era of William McKinley**

Mark Hanna and William McKinley

William McKinley as President of the United States

William McKinley as an Ohio politician

William McKinley and the Spanish-American War of 1898

William McKinley in political cartoons

Some Photographs and images of William McKinley

The Era of William McKinley

http://www.cohums.ohio-state.edu/
history/projects/McKinley/

Political cartoons, photographic images, and the Spanish-American War are but a few of the interesting links from this historic site.

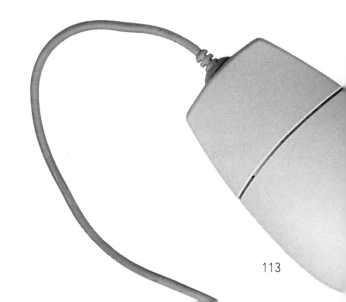

Imperialism and the Philippines

Although William McKinley was one of the kindest and most peace-loving Presidents to date, circumstances and national pressures resulted in U. S. participation in more than one conflict. Following the Spanish-American War, the United States was in possession of Guam, Puerto Rico, and the Philippines.

Debates took place about whether the United States would be perceived as imperialist by holding on to these spoils of war. Some argued that the territories were too distant and would require large resources to maintain. Others argued that they should be kept as the spoils of war. Although he had great misgivings, McKinley finally conceded to the proponents and decided to acquire these territories.

Objective

Students will be able to describe how the United States acquired the islands of Guam, Puerto Rico, and the Philippines and how their acquisition was viewed as imperialism. Students will be able to locate the islands of Guam, Puerto Rico, and the Philippines on a map.

Time Required

1 hour

Materials

- Writing materials
- Atlas
- World maps
- Internet access
- Calculators
- Library access

Procedure

Have students form debate teams, researching and preparing for debate that would argue the issues—e.g., is the victor entitled to occupy the conquered territories? Is this as true today as it was historically? What factors are involved in the decision whether to occupy conquered territories and how occupation is perceived?

Students will identify the three territories on a map and will calculate time and distance to reach these areas. The calculations might include shipping vessels from the McKinley era as well as commercial and military aircraft of today.

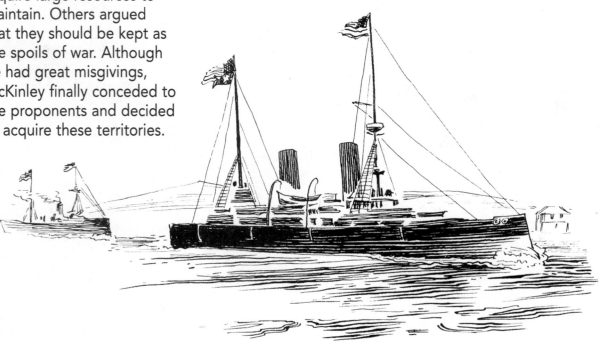

A Standard That Was Truly Gold

During the early 1890s, most countries were on the gold standard. In 1900 a law made gold the standard for U. S. currency. This meant that a stated amount of gold could be exchanged for paper money at any national bank or the U. S. treasury. At that time, each paper dollar had a gold value of 1.67 grams of gold. Although the gold standard was abandoned in 1933, it remained as a standard of measurement into the 1970s. Now the price and value of gold rises and falls on what is known as the "gold markets."

Objective
Students will be able to describe the gold standard and use a facsimile of gold to calculate the worth of past and present currency.

Time Required
1 hour

Materials
- Weighing scales
- Weights
- Gold facsimile (small rocks painted gold)
- Writing materials
- Reading material related to the gold standard
- Internet access to the gold trading exchange

Procedure
Students will be given (or they may discover gold) pieces of gold facsimile to weigh and determine value according to the pre-1933 gold standard. As well, they can check the gold markets using a financial news site on the Internet (e.g., CNN) and calculate the value of the gold they possess. Simulate changing conditions in the world economy that can change the value of gold and cause fortunes to be won and lost. A debriefing session should follow, with full documentation on classroom charts and graphs.

Extensions
1. The Klondike Gold Rush was on. How did it differ from that of the California Gold Rush? Which one would you have wanted to participate in and why?

2. Trace as many Spanish influences still present in the Philippines as possible. Where specifically can their origins be traced? How and when did they arrive on the islands?

3. A proper handshake is a part of western culture. President McKinley is thought to hold the record for presidential handshaking, meeting and shaking hands with as many as twenty-five hundred people in one hour. Teach the proper form of the handshake and practice at school and at home.

26th President

Theodore Roosevelt
1901 - 1909

Theodore Roosevelt achieved great popularity both at home and abroad. Enhancing his reputation was his winning the Nobel Peace Prize for his role as arbitrator in the Russo-Japanese War and his work as a conservationist, in which he was effective in adding a great deal of land to the national forests, designating public land use, and supporting needed irrigation projects.

Theodore Roosevelt

http://www.ipl.org/ref/POTUS/troosevelt.html

Whether you're learning about "Trust Buster Teddy" or "Mr. President," this page has it all. A graduate from Harvard College, a member of the Dutch Reformed Church, and a former governor of New York are but a few of the interesting facts about the life of Theodore Roosevelt found on this site.

Selected Works of Theodore Roosevelt, New Bartleby Library

http://www.bartleby.com/tr/

This site shares some of Theodore Roosevelt's writings and thoughts on various personal topics, offering a further glimpse into the life of this famous man.

Panama Canal

http://www.pancanal.com

The Panama Canal changed shipping, travel, commerce, and defense in the Western Hemisphere. One of the greatest construction projects of all time, the Panama Canal is a proud and practical water highway serving all ocean-going peoples of the world.

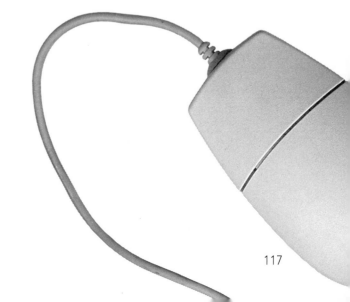

Mottoes for All Occasions

Theodore Roosevelt coined a slogan for his foreign affairs policies. When we say "speak softly but carry a big stick," historians know we are referring to Teddy Roosevelt.

Objective
Students will be able to identify and write mottoes that have significant meaning.

Time Required
1 1/2 hours

Materials
• Internet access
• Library resources
• Paper
• Pencils

Procedure
Discuss political slogans or mottoes and their historical origins. Give the class examples. Discover how political cartoons are often the origin of slogans. Each student will research a President, finding important and unusual facts about his term in office.

After writing those events, characteristics, or facts on paper, students will write a motto that is representative of that President. An example might be the

Theodore Roosevelt motto, or one we could write for Jimmy Carter: "A peanut farmer at home, a humanitarian at heart."

After students write the slogan or motto for their assigned President, they should illustrate the motto with a picture or draw a captioned cartoon. Share the finished slogan/mottoes and display them.

The Big Canal

Following the independence of Panama in 1903 and the recognition of the new republic, the Hay-Bunau-Varilla Treaty was signed. This treaty called for the creation of the Panama Canal Zone, and construction of the canal began in 1904. Viewed as one of the major engineering feats at the turn of the century, this lock canal created an important man-made waterway across the Isthmus of Panama connecting the Pacific and Atlantic oceans.

PANAMA CANAL ZONE

Objective
Students will design and build a canal lock system similar to those used in the Panama Canal.

Time Required
Three sessions of 40 minutes each

Materials
- Sturdy cardboard
- Scissors
- Pencils
- Paint
- Duct tape
- Internet access

Procedure
Following the study of the Panama Canal, show students various photos, drawings, schematics, etc., of the lock system that enables the canal to operate. Several good videos are available, as are Internet sites. Have two or three teams of students design a three-tier lock system, drawing their plans on paper.

Students should meet with you to defend their plans. Once you have approved the designs, students will select the materials for construction. Construction of the locks might require one or two sessions. Once the system is completed, the locks may be painted or colored. Display with the original plans for all to see and study.

Extensions
1. Yellow fever was an unexpected danger faced by workers on the Panama Canal. What was it, and why did it affect the foreign worker but not those who lived in the area?

2. Most of us have had a Teddy bear. What do you think the origin of this toy might be? Students can look for representative samples of real Teddy bears, old and new.

3. In 1906 Roosevelt was awarded the Nobel Peace Prize for arbitrating the end of the Russo-Japanese War. What is the Nobel Peace Prize, and what is the history of this unusual and prestigious award?

27th President

William H. Taft
1909 – 1913

William Howard Taft found himself a candidate for President in what would become a personal time of awkwardness and discontent. Taft, who much preferred practicing law to national politics, later served proudly as the Chief Justice of the United States.

Cherry Blossoms in Washington

http://www.nps.gov/nacc/cherry/index.htm

Any springtime visitor to Washington, D.C., will marvel at the beauty of the famous cherry blossoms that cast a pink spell over the city. For each blossom that touches our senses, we can thank Helen Taft, First Lady, who had the Japanese Cherry trees planted. This site shares the history and beauty of these special and delicate trees with the people of the nation.

It's Tax Time: The History of the Sixteenth Amendment

http://www.cats.org/16hist.html

The Sixteenth Amendment to the Constitution was ratified during Taft's administration. The story of this unusual legislation, still debated every April 15, is found in this special IRS file.

William H. Taft

http://www.whitehouse.gov/WH/glimpse/presidents/html/wt27.html

President Taft was a reluctant candidate for the office of President. He preferred law to politics, and many say this was reflected in his actions as President. This site contains interesting facts about this very large man.

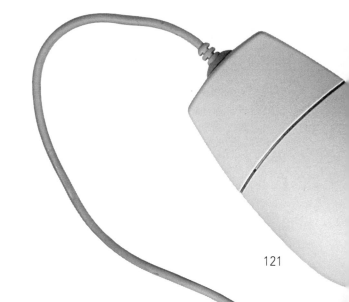

Taxes, Taxes, Taxes

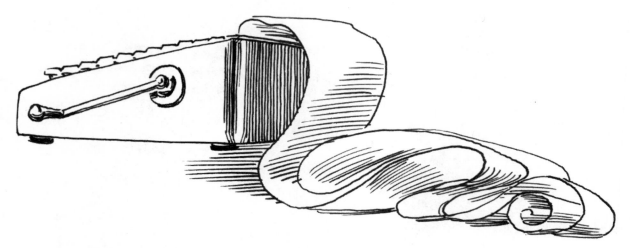

The Sixteenth Amendment to the Constitution of the United States was ratified on February 25, 1913. It gave Congress the power to impose taxation on the income of individuals and corporations by stating that "Congress shall have power to lay and collect taxes on incomes, from whatever sources derived, without apportionment among the several States, and without regard to any census or enumeration."

Objective

Students will participate in a classroom taxation project that will reveal the nature of taxation for government services.

Time Required

1 day
30 minutes for debriefing

Materials

- Internet access
- Library resources
- Paper
- Pencils
- One thousand tokens (printed from computer and cut apart)

Procedure

Introduce students to the concept of taxation for government services by giving each student fifty tokens as a starting point. Give them extra tokens for work performed in the class. Job assignments need not be equitable, nor does the number of tokens for the same job (e.g., a new teacher would receive fewer than a teacher with twenty years of experience). Assess tokens from students for services rendered, or they may be taken as an equal assessment from all members of the class. To pay for the drinking fountain, all students will be equally assessed whether they use it or not. Recess will receive an equal assessment from all students. Sharpening pencils will be an individual assessment, as will using a calculator or the classroom computer. After a full day of being assessed and earning tokens, the students will first list their feelings about being taxed for services and then discuss what would happen if there were no taxes. The discussion could extend to what the class feels are fair taxes and those they feel are unfair or not needed.

It's Cherry Blossom Time (or Some Other Tree)

As a tribute to the new relationship with Japan, Helen Taft succeeded in having the Japanese cherry trees planted in Washington. For many years, the trees have been both a tourist attraction and one of the wonders of this important city.

Objective
Students will be able to describe how trees enhance the physical environment of a city. Students will plant a tree at the school.

Time Required
1 hour of discussion, research, and decision making
1 hour for planting a tree
30 minutes for a dedication ceremony

Materials
• Sturdy material
• Internet access
• Selected tree
• Planting instructions
• Tools
• Planting mulch
• Water
• Hose

Procedure
Have students view many cities via the Internet to determine the vegetative environment of each. View images from around the world and discuss the types of landscaping used to enhance the beauty of an area. Based on climate, precipitation, and care requirements, select an attractive tree to plant on the school grounds. Contact a local nursery for instructions on the care and handling of the sapling. Organize a school assembly to celebrate the planting.

Extensions
1. New Mexico and Arizona were admitted to the Union in 1912. What were the circumstances of their admission, and why were they important to the formation of the country? When one country gains territory, another loses territory. What did this loss represent to whom?

2. Write to a congressional Representative or Senator and ask about his or her position on increased or decreased taxation.

3. Bring in an artifact from nineteenth-century Japan.

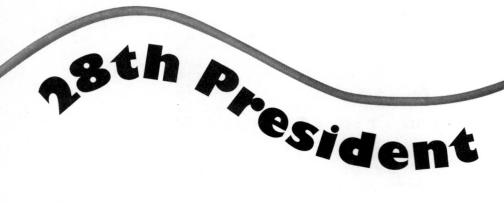

28th President

Woodrow Wilson
1913 – 1921

Woodrow Wilson viewed himself as the personal representative of the people. As such, he developed programs of progressive reform at home while building his reputation as a world leader by participating in constructing the armistice agreement that ended World War I.

World War I Document Archive

http://www.lib.byu.edu/~rdh/wwi/index.html

World War I was supposed to be the last war. The United States embarked on war against Germany during Woodrow Wilson's second term in office. This site contains primary documents from World War I archives. Search within the site and move on to related links.

From School Master to President

http://www.ipl.org/ref/POTUS/wwilson.html

The "School Master in Politics" became President and served two tumultuous terms in the early part of the twentieth century. This site reviews many of the people, places, and events of that period.

Votes for Women
1850-1920

http://lcweb2.loc.gov/ammem/
vfwhtml/vfwhome.html

This site reviews the events of approximately a hundred years leading up to suffrage. It includes text and great photos.

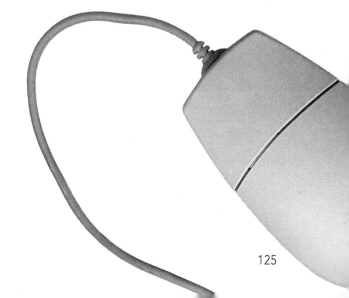

Lessons for Learning

The First War of the World

Although President Wilson sought to remain neutral during the war in Europe, events brought the United States closer to the conflict. The sinking of the British liner *Lusitania* by a German submarine with more than a thousand lives lost (more than one hundred were Americans), convinced Wilson that U. S. involvement could no longer be avoided. On April 2, 1917, Congress declared war on Germany.

Objective

Students will be able to describe how the United States entered into the First World War, name the countries involved, map their locations and distances, and collect other pertinent information. Students will write journal entries relating feelings and fears about fighting in a war far away from home.

Time Required

Three sessions of 1 hour each

Materials

- Internet access
- Library resources
- Maps
- Calculators
- Writing materials

Procedure

Hang a world map on a bulletin board in the classroom. Instruct students to locate the countries involved in World War I. Using their home town as a point of reference, and with the help of the scale on the map, determine how far the countries are from the United States.

Ask students to imagine themselves as soldiers far away from home for the first time, fighting in a place where they don't speak the language. Have students write three journal entries describing the experience. Journals may be shared with the class in a quiet and peaceful setting.

The Nobel Prize

First awarded in 1901, the Nobel Prize acknowledges those individuals or a group of individuals who have bestowed "the greatest benefit on mankind." Awarded in the areas of literature, physiology or medicine, physics, chemistry, and peace, Woodrow Wilson won the Nobel Peace Prize for 1919 largely due to his efforts in the establishment of a League of Nations.

Objective

Students will be able to describe why President Wilson received the Nobel Peace Prize. Students will be able to identify the origins of the Nobel Peace Prize. Students will present a special award to a recipient in the community or school for outstanding deeds.

Time Required

Three sessions of 1 hour each

Materials

- Award-maker computer program
- Research and writing materials

Procedure

Following the study of Alfred Nobel, the Nobel Peace Prize, and relevant past recipients, ask students to identify a person from the community or school (adult or student) who is deemed to be worthy of receiving a special award. Students should submit their nominations in writing with a brief summary describing the nominee's character and attributes. Organize a panel of students, parents, and teachers to review the nominations and to make the selections.

Using a computer award-maker program, students will design and print awards for the individuals selected. A special classroom assembly should be organized with invitations, honored guests, dignitaries, etc., for this special recognition.

Extensions

1. It's tax time. Income tax is now a part of American life. Students can access the Internal Revenue page for information or to download tax forms. With fictitious income data, students can calculate taxes due the federal government. Discuss what taxes provide.

2. In 1920, the Nineteenth Amendment to the Constitution, giving women the right to vote, was ratified. Since the War of Independence took place one hundred fifty years earlier, why did it take so long for this to occur? Have your class research the issue from the perspective of those living at the time, and debate the pros and cons of this amendment. What would life be like in the United States today if woman did not have the right to vote?

3. President Wilson was the first President who had earned a Ph.D. Discover what these letters represent and how a Ph.D. is obtained. Do you know anyone with a Ph.D.?

29th President

Warren G. Harding
1921 – 1923

Following World War I, President Warren Harding proclaimed, "America's present need is not heroics, but healing; not nostrums, but normalcy; not revolution, but adjustment; restoration, not agitation . . . not submergence in internationality, but sustainment in triumphant nationality. . . ."

American Leaders Speak from the Library of Congress

http://lcweb2.loc.gov/

"The American Memory" Warren Harding site provides a closer look at the new Americanism, new nationalism, the League of Nations, and liberty under the law. To access the collection, type "Harding" in the search box.

Teapot Dome Scandal

http://www.grolier.com/presidents/ea/side/teapot.html

As a result of the Teapot Dome Scandal and other scandals that would follow, the trust in the credibility of the Harding administration suffered. This site highlights this particular scandal and offers the student a look at government in action.

[Text version]

Warren G. Harding
Twenty-Ninth President 1921-1923

[Florence Kling Harding]

Warren G. Harding

http://www.whitehouse.gov/WH/
glimpse/presidents/html/wh29.html

Quotas on immigration, new tariffs, and the great coal strikes of 1921 were among the experiences of the twenty-ninth President of the United States. This site reviews the many events and accomplishments of President Harding.

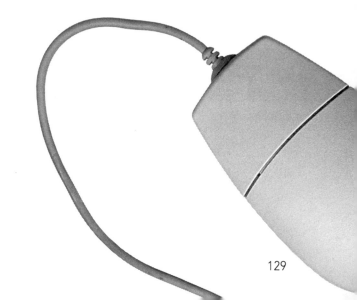

The Immigration Reduction Act of 1921

- If not admitted, will be imprisoned as a political prisoner
- Family will be separated and will live their lives apart
- Will starve on the streets of [name of your city or town]
- Will be conscripted into the armed forces and will be killed in action
- Will work on a farm and raise a family of six children
- Will immigrate to Australia and become successful in a small business
- Will settle in Argentina

Insert the cards into envelopes and distribute them randomly to members of the class. The students will not look at the cards until you tell them to do so. Set quotas, such as the following: Only two people with pink cards may enter the United States; five people who hold brown cards may enter; but only one person with a red card may enter. Those that enter will be seated on one end of the room, while those who were not admitted will be seated in another area.

Students will take turns reading what happens to them because of the restrictions on immigration. The teacher can chart the actions for each individual and group. Debriefing or process feedback should follow.

During the Harding administration, the government imposed restrictions on the number of immigrants allowed to enter the United States. Quotas were established as a way to reduce the numbers entering the country from foreign nations.

Objective

Students will participate in an immigration simulation to understand the Immigration Reduction Act of 1921.

Time Required

1 hour

Materials

- Simulation materials
- Cards
- Envelopes
- Construction paper of different colors

Procedure

Cut three-by-five-inch colored construction paper into stacks of five sheets each, with each stack a different color. For a class of thirty, there should be six stacks. Each card in the distinct color stack should be labeled with the name of an immigrant group from the period. On the reverse side of the card, state such conditions as:

Meet the President

President Harding loved to meet with the public. He would greet almost everyone who came to visit. Of course, it is much more difficult today to see the President in person, let alone actually meet him.

Objective

Students will be able to describe the limited access the public has to the President today. Students will attempt to increase access to our current President.

Time Required

45 minutes

Materials

- Historical materials
- Photographs of the public meeting with the President
- Writing materials

Procedure

Students will discover which individuals and groups have access to the President. They will discuss what could be done to increase their access. Instruct students to draft a class letter that includes pictures and something unique about a current area of study and invite the President to visit the next time he is in town. Using conventional mail or e-mail, send the letter to the President. The class might want to explore what happens prior to and during a presidential visit. When (or if) a reply is received, determine the next step of the activity based on the response. You may have to prepare for a presidential visit! This should be quite a learning experience.

Extensions

1. President Harding was the first President to own a radio at the White House. What do you think Harding listened to? Ask a grandparent or senior citizen if he or she listened to the radio when young. What programs did they tune in to? Have the students explore the varied radio programming available today.

2. This was the period of baseball's Negro Leagues. Why did these leagues form, who was on the teams, and who were the stars? This is an interesting epic of social, cultural, and sports history.

3. Harding ordered troops into West Virginia during a coal miners' strike in 1921. Coal mining was back-breaking and dangerous work. The United States was in a period of rapid growth and had developed a great dependence on coal. What was coal used for? Why was it so important? How was coal extracted? Why was the work of miners so dangerous? Do we still have coal miners today?

30th President

Calvin Coolidge
1923 – 1929

Calvin Coolidge attempted to preserve traditional, moral, and economic ideals amid the newly emerging material and social prosperity that swept America during his term.

Roaring Twenties

http://sunsite.unc.edu/lia/president/
HooverLibrary/museum/
Museum-Guide3.html

Coolidge was in office during the Roaring Twenties. It was a time of jazz, Wall Street speculation, Hollywood, and woman's suffrage. The times were exciting, and the nation was on the move again.

Calvin Coolidge

http://publishing.grolier.com/
presidents/ea/bios/30pcool.html

If you want to learn about "Silent Cal," this is the place to be. Born on the Fourth of July in 1872, this Independence Day baby would grow up to be the President of the United States.

RYAN NYP "SPIRIT OF ST. LOUIS"

First Nonstop Solo Transatlantic Flight

62k GIF - 35k JPEG
© 1987 Smithsonian Institution
photo #79-780 by M. Avino

On May 21, 1927, Charles A. Lindbergh completed the first solo nonstop transatlantic flight in history, flying his **Ryan NYP "Spirit of St. Louis"** 5,810 kilometers (3,610 miles) between Roosevelt Field on Long Island, New York, and Paris, France, in 33 hours, 30 minutes. With this flight, Lindbergh won the $25,000 prize offered by New York hotel owner Raymond Orteig to the first aviator to fly an aircraft directly across the Atlantic between New York and Paris. When he landed at Le Bourget Field in Paris, Lindbergh became a world hero who would remain in the public eye for decades.

The aftermath of the flight was the "Lindbergh boom" in aviation: aircraft industry stocks rose in value and interest in flying skyrocketed. Lindbergh's subsequent U.S. tour in the "Spirit of St. Louis" demonstrated the potential of the airplane as a safe, reliable mode of transportation. Following the U.S. tour, Lindbergh took the aircraft on a goodwill flight to Central and South America, where flags of the countries he visited were painted

Charles Lindbergh, The Spirit Moved Us All

http://www.nasm.edu/GALLERIES/
GAL100/stlouis.html

Charles Lindbergh and his *Spirit of St. Louis* captured the attention of America when he set out to do what no one had ever accomplished. The world watched and listened as Lindbergh flew from New York to Paris to capture the record and the hearts of all people.

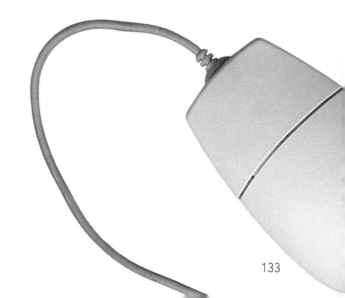

Lessons for Learning

They Were the Roaring Twenties

The Roaring Twenties was a period like none other in American history. The county was obsessed with opposites—such as temperance and speakeasies. It was a time of opulence, adventure, outrageousness, and uncertainty. Historians can interpret the 1920s in a variety of ways, depending on the perspective from which the period is viewed.

Objective
Students will construct a collage depicting the dress, culture, style and events of the Roaring Twenties.

Time Required
1 1/2 hours

Materials
• Internet access
• Library resources
• Newspapers
• Magazines
• Writing materials

Procedure
In this class, students will make a collage depicting their perception of the period, based on data collected. Provide students with pictorials, photocopies, downloadable photographs, advertisements, etc., that offer varying views of the period. Students will select those artifacts they deem appropriate to be placed in their collage. At the completion of the art history project, discuss and display the products.

The <u>Spirit of St. Louis</u>

This was a time of progress, color, and drama. Perhaps it makes sense that Charles Lindbergh, alone in his single-engine plane, did what no one had been able to do before him. A great aviation pioneer, he piloted his craft, *Spirit of St. Louis*, nonstop across the Atlantic to an airstrip just outside of Paris, France. Today the plane that Lindbergh flew hangs proudly in the Air and Space Museum of the Smithsonian Institution in Washington, D.C.

Objective
Students will be able to participate in a simulated flight with Charles Lindbergh in the airplane *Spirit of St. Louis*.

Time Required
1 hour per student per week

Materials
• Internet access
• Research and writing materials
• E-mail
• Large box

Procedure
Determine the size of the cockpit of the *Spirit of St. Louis*. Out of large appliance boxes, construct a replica (in terms of size) of the space inside the plane. Allow students to sit in the box for an hour and see if they can imagine how Lindbergh must have felt, through light and dark, during his thirty-three-hour flight.

Extensions
1. "The Babe," Babe Ruth, was the star of baseball. Research his salary compared to what the President of the country was earning. Compare the salaries of sports stars today with those of the President. What conclusions can you draw?

2. The 1920s ushered in the first motion picture animated film. Have students design and construct a flip book providing graphic examples of animation.

3. A revolution was smoldering far to the south of the United States. Most people had never heard of the country called Nicaragua. Where is it and what makes it unique?

31st President

Herbert C. Hoover
1929 – 1933

Herbert Hoover, whose public career spanned fifty years, was elected as the Chief Executive of the United States in 1929. After his term in office, presidents Truman and Eisenhower asked him to again serve his country as a member of various government commissions.

The Great Depression

http://www.escape.com/~paulg53/politics/great_depression.shtml

From the excitement and music of the Roaring Twenties to the apple stands and soup kitchens of the Thirties, the Great Depression changed lives forever.

It All Came Crashing Down: The Stock Market Crash of 1929

http://www.magma.ca/~davef/crash29.html

The Stock Market Crash of 1929 heralded possibly the greatest economic depression of all time. Learn more about this worldwide event, and decide whether it could happen again.

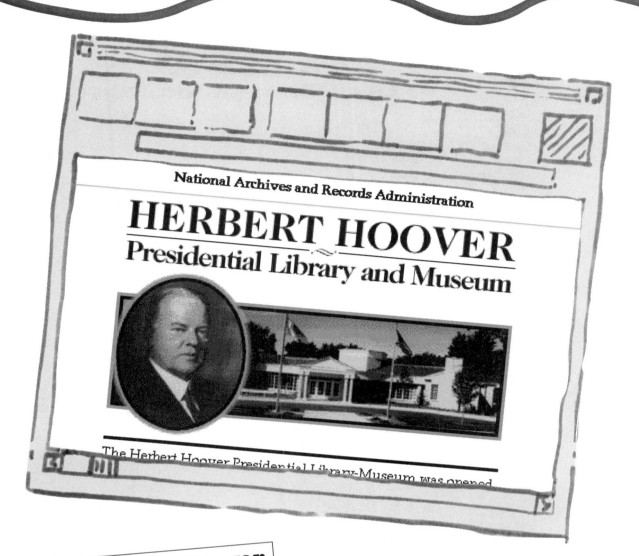

National Archives and Records Administration

HERBERT HOOVER
Presidential Library and Museum

The Herbert Hoover Presidential Library-Museum was opened

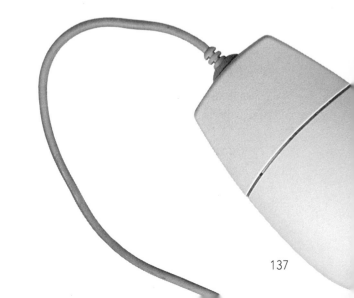

The Herbert Hoover Presidential Library

http://www.hoover.nara.gov

Orphaned at age nine, Herbert Clark Hoover rose to become thirty-first President of the United States. This site is a tour through the Herbert Hoover Library, a special place that records the history of the man and his manners. The visitor can peruse the "stacks" or e-mail the curators. Visit as often as you wish; the admission is free.

I Lived Through the Depression

Although sparked by the Stock Market Crash of 1929, the Great Depression had its roots deeply planted long before the crash occurred. There were serious economic problems in major industries, such as agriculture, mining, construction, railroads, and textiles, which provided employment for the nation's large workforce. Thousands of banks and businesses failed. The crash of the stock market heralded difficult times.

Objective
Students will engage in an oral history lesson by studying the era of the Great Depression and then interviewing a person who lived through this time of history.

Time Required
Two sessions of 1 hour each for introduction and reading
30 minutes per interview
Class presentation to be arranged

Materials
• Internet access
• Library resources
• Newspaper archives
• Audio tape
• Audio recorder
• Writing materials

Procedure
Have students view videotapes and read books and other literary accounts of the Great Depression. When they have an understanding of this time, ask students to work in teams to identify an individual who lived through this period and who will consent to a recorded oral interview. Students will formulate questions, test equipment, make appointments, and complete the interview. Some transcription may be necessary. This should be a rich lesson that brings a primary source into the classroom via audio technology.

One Dust Bowl—Hold the Rain

When the South and Midwest experienced a drought in the late 1920s and early 1930s, a tragic set of events occurred. The land continued to dry and crack, and when the hot winds blew, the earth turned into dust. With no precipitation to cement the dirt in place, the hot winds lifted the top layers of soil and cast it to the skies. Nothing would grow, and the rich topsoils were lost.

Objective

Students will be able to describe the ecological events that caused the famous dust bowl in Oklahoma and the Midwest.

Time Required

Several 1-hour sessions for set-up
10 minutes each day to grow plants and simulation

Materials

- Internet access
- Research and writing materials
- E-mail

Procedure

Have your students create a small dust bowl so that they can see the effects of water, wind, and heat on the soil. Cut down two cardboard boxes so that they have sides of about three inches. Fill the boxes with a very light soil. Plant some fast-growing seeds like beans or grass in rows within the boxes. Set the boxes outside during the day if weather permits. Water both boxes until the plants sprout. Continue to water one box while letting the other box dry out. Using a household fan and extension cord (be sure to use caution), turn the fan on low so that it blows on the dry box. Soon the soil will begin to turn to fine dust and blow away, leaving only the rocks and poor soil at the bottom. This is similar to what occurred in Oklahoma. As a result of the dust bowls, the people of the region began their migration to California, looking for a new life.

Extensions

1. When the stock market plunged in 1929, fortunes were lost, and the United States fell deeper into economic depression. The stock market is a place where the public can purchase shares in businesses and corporations. Have students select stocks to "purchase" on one of the exchanges. They can use the daily newspaper to select the stocks. They can then use Internet financial sites to chart the progress of the stocks on a daily basis. Be sure to post charts and graphs so everyone can keep up to date.

2. As an honored and respected President, Herbert Hoover received dozens of keys to many cities. The phrase "We offer you the keys to the city" has been used often at ceremonies honoring some important individual. What does this really mean? Who has been given the key to your city in recent times? How would you find out?

3. During the Great Depression, unemployment hit a record with nearly 25 percent of the population, or one in every four people, was out of work. Today the unemployment rate is much lower—in the single digits. Demonstrate with your class the effect of 25 percent during the Depression as compared with the effect of the current rate. Have students move to the sides of the room if they have been designated unemployed. How will they feed, clothe, and provide shelter for their families?

32nd President

Franklin D. Roosevelt
1933 – 1945

Franklin D. Roosevelt earned the distinction of being elected to the presidency an unprecedented four times. From the New Deal to World War II, his continued popularity and political astuteness influenced the future of American society.

The History Place: World War II in Europe and the Pacific

http://www.historyplace.com/worldwar2/timeline/ww2time.htm

http://www.historyplace.com/united-states/pacificwar/index.html

These comprehensive sites contain time lines and resources related to the European and Pacific campaigns of World War II.

Franklin D. Roosevelt

http://www.ipl.org/ref/POTUS/fdroosevelt.html

The thirty-second President of the United States served longer than any other President. In this biographical and event site, the visitor can access the many data and photo links that record this truly remarkable leader.

Franklin Roosevelt

http://tlc.ai.org/froosidx.htm

Join us as we chronicle FDR from the Great Depression and The New Deal to World War II. This comprehensive site offers numerous fascinating links related to this unusual President with the longest tenure in the Oval Office.

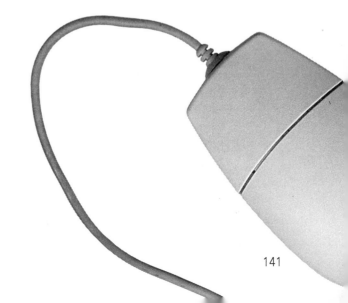

The New Deal, Relief, and Recovery

The Civilian Conservation Corps (CCC) was one of many solutions intended to help reconstruct the country's economic base following the Great Depression. The CCC, along with the Army Corps of Engineers and other groups, worked on forest conservation projects, roads, and bridges, building a stronger national infrastructure.

Objective
Students will design and construct model bridges.

Time Required
Two sessions of 1 hour each

Materials
• Backing board
• Straws
• Toothpicks
• Cardboard
• Glue
• Rubber bands

Procedure
Students will attempt to construct their own bridges using the materials and ideas presented. Show students many pictures of road spans, trestles, and miscellaneous bridges. Discuss the common and unique engineering features of the bridges presented. Demonstrate the use of a geometric design and how multiple triangles are stronger than rectangles. Through an inquiry process have the students discover the reasons.

Divide students into teams and provide them with the bridge materials. Demonstrate some of the possibilities and construction techniques (glue application, tying, geometric shapes, use of rubber bands, etc.). Let the construction begin.

New - World - Telegram   WALL ST.

ROOSEVELT and the NEW DEAL: On the Road to Recovery

World Leaders of the Time

During World War II, the world witnessed the emergence of powerful and influential leaders whose decisions altered the course of history and changed the lives of millions of people. Franklin D. Roosevelt, Winston Churchhill, Benito Mussolini, Joseph Stalin, Emperor Hirohito of Japan, and Adolf Hilter all played pivotal roles in this global confrontation.

Objective
Using a Venn diagram, students will be able to demonstrate graphically the similarities and differences related to world leaders of the time.

Time Required
1 hour

Materials
- Venn diagram template (Quad Venn)
- Research materials
- Internet and library access

Procedure
Following a discussion of the period of study, have students do research using library and/or Internet resources to learn more about the leaders of this period. They may wish to study Roosevelt, Hitler, Stalin, Churchill, and others. They should first make lists of the personal and leadership characteristics of these leaders, later transferring them to the Venn diagrams. At completion, students can write a brief summary that they attach to the Venn diagram, mounting it for display.

Extensions
1. What evidence exists today of the agencies created during the Roosevelt years?

2. In Washington, D.C., a monument was erected to recognize the accomplishments of President Roosevelt. What other monuments were constructed in Washington to immortalize previous leaders?

3. One of the world's greatest tragedies and crimes against humanity was the Holocaust carried out by Germany in World War II. This event has been portrayed in many ways through movies, photos, letters, documentaries, oral history, and art. Have your students locate art from the Holocaust that was painted or drawn by some of the thousands of child victims.

33rd President

Harry S. Truman
1945 – 1953

Harry S. Truman, an honest and straightforward President, would lead the world into peace after World War II, the most devastating conflict of all time. As the chief commander, Truman authorized the use of atomic weapons on civilian targets to bring an end to the war in the Pacific.

The City of Hiroshima

http://www.city.hiroshima.jp/

This Japanese site has links to the atomic bomb and peace information that will be of interest to those who ask questions about this troubled period.

Harry S. Truman

http://www2.whitehouse.gov/WH/glimpse/presidents/html/ht33.html

This information page introduces the thirty-third President of the United States as he assumed the difficult task of bringing World War II to a close and fighting a new war with a much different foe.

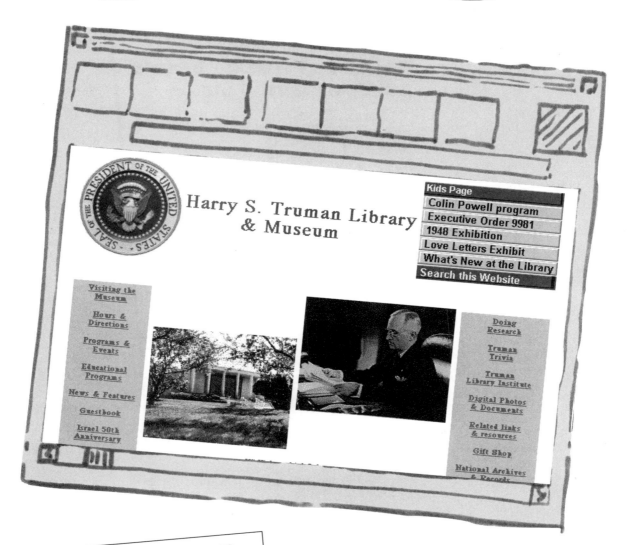

Kids Page
Colin Powell program
Executive Order 9981
1948 Exhibition
Love Letters Exhibit
What's New at the Library
Search this Website

Harry S. Truman Library
& Museum

Visiting the Museum

Hours & Directions

Programs & Events

Educational Programs

News & Features

Guestbook

Israel 50th Anniversary

Doing Research

Truman Trivia

Truman Library Institute

Digital Photos & Documents

Related links & resources

Gift Shop

National Archives & Records

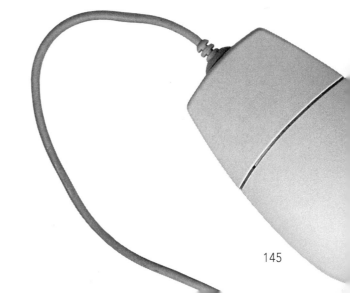

Harry S. Truman Library

http://www.lbjlib.utexas.edu/truman/

The Harry S. Truman Library and Museum serves as a repository of historical documents and artifacts for use by both scholars and the public. A view of Truman's life and Truman trivia are contained on this site.

Peaceful Use of War's Destructive Power

The atomic bomb was created secretly in the desert of New Mexico and was later dropped on the cities of Hiroshima and Nagasaki, Japan, to end the war in the Pacific. The nuclear energy that made possible the most destructive weapon known to mankind has made a postwar reappearance for peaceful purposes.

Objective

Students will be able to describe the many peaceful uses of nuclear energy that was first used as a destructive instrument of war.

Required Time

Two sessions of 1 hour each

Materials

- Internet access
- Library access
- Writing materials

Procedure

Nuclear energy has been harnessed to operate electrical power plants, to fuel giant ocean-going ships, and to desalinate ocean water. Have your students explore one of these or other peacetime uses of nuclear energy. They can complete comprehensive projects with text, pictures, and models related to operation, location, and possible future use. The future angle could prove very interesting and motivating. These projects might be very appropriate to display at a science fair, open house, or special presentation to the community.

The United Nations for World Peace

It was during the Truman administration that the United Nations organization was formed to forever end the possibility of another world conflict. The United Nations is intended to resolve issues and conflicts, promote human rights, and offer economic development throughout the world.

Objective

Students will be able to describe the United Nations and develop a profile of one member nation.

Time Required

Three sessions of 1 hour each
Independent homework

Materials

- Internet access
- Library access
- Letter-writing materials
- Writing materials

Procedure

Have your students make a list of current United Nations member countries. From the list, a student can select one country about which he or she will do a comprehensive study and report. This report can be presented in traditional format, or on a technology-based format such as HyperStudio. Students may also wish to send letters to the many consulates of member countries requesting travel brochures and information. The projects will offer a current picture of the member country. When all projects are complete, display them in a magnificent and colorful mosaic throughout the classroom.

Extensions

1. After agreeing on an international issue of concern and understanding the workings of the world organization, students may wish to debate the issue in a model United Nations setting. The classroom can be reorganized to resemble the seating of the Security Council, and nameplates of member countries can be affixed to desks. This could be a week-long activity that will not soon be forgotten.

2. What is ENIAC? Your students will be astounded by the size of and energy use of this first computer. Occupying a large building of thousands of vacuum tubes, and consuming great amounts of energy, it had less power than an Apple IIe. Have your students explore and re-create in creative movement the workings of ENIAC.

3. The conflicting postwar philosophies between the democracies of the West and the communist governments of the East created what Winston Churchill called the "Iron Curtain." Although a war between the superpowers of the United States and the Soviet Union was never fought, the "Cold War" of words threatened the world and continued for decades. Have your students explore the Cold War from the perspective of someone who was living between 1950 and 1990. See if you know anyone who installed a bomb shelter in their backyard.

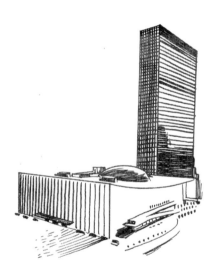

34th President

Dwight D. Eisenhower
1953 – 1961

Dwight D. Eisenhower, a well-known U. S. Army General, would emerge to lead the nation during the onset of what became known as the new Cold War. Anticommunism at home and abroad became the new political focus that divided and shook the nation as never before.

Dwight D. Eisenhower

http://www.whitehouse.gov/WH/glimpse/presidents/html/de34.html

As President, General Dwight D. Eisenhower, a decorated leader in World War II, declared the "Nation's desire for world peace." From election slogans like "I Like Ike" to the putting green installed on the White House lawn, this site focuses on his goal of securing a lasting world peace.

Dwight D. Eisenhower Presidential Library

http://sunsite.unc.edu/lia/president/eisenhower.html

Visit the Dwight D. Eisenhower Presidential Library to find text, photos, and information about our nation's leader.

THE MONTGOMERY BUS BOYCOTT PAGE

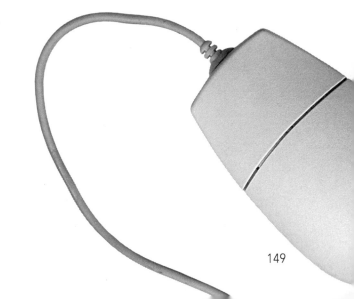

The Montgomery Bus Boycott Page

http://socsci.colorado.edu/
~jonesem/montgomery.html

Although history records President Eisenhower as sympathetic to desegregating the schools and armed forces, protests in the cities were reinforcing the need for quicker social change. This site sheds light on Rosa Parks and the Montgomery bus boycott, bringing this period into perspective.

Lessons for Learning

The Blacklist

Hysteria against Communism emerged during the Truman and Eisenhower administrations. A committee led by Senator Joseph R. McCarthy attempted to uncover suspected communists throughout American society. Individuals accused by McCarthy were often "blacklisted" and prevented from working in their given fields. Most were innocent people whose careers were ruined. The term "McCarthyism" now refers to extraordinary and sensational personal attacks based on unverified charges.

Objective

Students will participate in class life regulated by a "blacklist" to understand the exclusion created by this dark period in our nation's history.

Time Required

Two sessions of 1 hour each

Materials

- Internet access
- Library resources
- Newspaper archives
- Videos of the House Committee on Un-American Activities hearings

Procedure

Compile a fictitious "secret" list of those with different views or with associates who have different views from the mainstream. Distribute six cards, each with brief background information about those being blacklisted. Create opportunities for jobs, travel, promotion, etc., to give to those who are not on the blacklist. Those whose names do appear on the list will be brought before a panel and questioned about all aspects of their lives.

Underscore this simulation with discussions, stories, and films related to this period of history. Ask the class to discuss the rationale for this political climate, the anticommunist agenda, and the various reactions that occurred. It is very important to hold a process debriefing at various times in this experience.

The Russians Were First

When the Russians launched the first orbiting spacecraft, *Sputnik*, into space in 1957, millions of people looked to the night sky to catch a glimpse of this man-made orbiter. In Washington, Eisenhower and his advisors were planning what would soon become known as the "space race."

Objective
Students will create a model *Sputnik* orbiting spacecraft.

Time Required
1 hour

Materials
- Internet access
- Styrofoam balls
- Egg cartons
- Balloons
- Papier-mâché
- Glue or glue sticks
- Tempera paint

Procedure
Share with students the history of the Russian *Sputnik* spacecraft and the nature of this truly remarkable accomplishment. Be sure to discuss the reaction of the United States.

Students can access one of the many Internet space sites and learn more about early space exploration and the intergalactic probes of today.

From that first orbiter evolved the first steps on the moon and all space exploration since.

As a celebration of this event, students may use the materials to design and construct a replica of the *Sputnik* space satellite. Once assembled, it can be decorated and readied for "flight." The objects can be suspended from the classroom ceiling as a tribute to this time in history.

Extensions
1. Eisenhower sent federal troops to Arkansas to protect the students and support the integration of Central High School. Are there still some public schools where racial integration has not occurred? Where are those schools? How is this possible? The answers might surprise you.

2. President Eisenhower, although thought of as a tough general, was also an accomplished chef and was famous for, among other things, his vegetable soup and pancakes. Have students make their own unique classroom version of vegetable soup. On another day, make corn pancakes with syrup.

3. In 1959 the National Aeronautics and Space Administration was established. Access the comprehensive NASA site on the World Wide Web and trace its history and current developments.

35th President

John F. Kennedy
1961 - 1963

A war hero with youth, charisma, and a background of wealth and influence, John F. Kennedy offered great hope to all Americans until his tragic assassination in Dallas, Texas. The event would rock the world and alter the face of history.

Inspiration, Youth, and Humor

http://www.ipl.org/ref/POTUS/jfkennedy.html

The young former PT 109 commander and U. S. Senator became the youngest person and the first Roman Catholic to be elected to the presidency. His few years in office proved to be both inspirational and difficult. This presidential Internet library provides insight into the life of the young President from Massachusetts.

John F. Kennedy Assassination Records Collection National Archives and Records Administration

http://www.nara.gov/nara/jfk/gil_42.html

The events that rocked the nation and the world on that November day in 1963 would raise questions and speculation to this day. This site provides powerful records of investigation and archival committees that sought answers to this tragic event.

OPERATIONS CENTER

FOURTEEN DAYS
IN OCTOBER:
THE CUBAN MISSILE CRISIS

Cuban Missile Crisis

http://hyperion.advanced.org/
11046/

The Operations Center examines
the fourteen days of the Cuban
Missile Crisis, which brought the
United States and the Soviet Union
close to nuclear conflict.

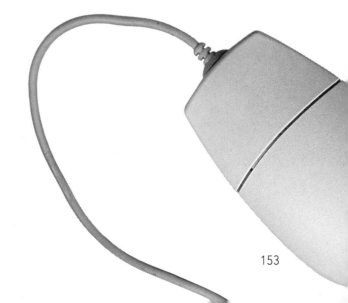

Lessons for Learning

The Peace Corps

The Peace Corps was a special project and a great accomplishment of President Kennedy's. It was intended to be a volunteer organization that carried goodwill, education, and occupational skill training to people in underdeveloped countries. The Peace Corps continues today in that same tradition.

Objective

Students will contact, via the Internet, a Peace Corps volunteer on another continent.

Time Required

1 hour on several different occasions

Materials

- Internet access
- Library resources
- Newspaper archives
- Videos and news spots related to the Peace Corps movement in the 1960s and today

Procedure

Peace Corps volunteers are often assigned to remote areas of Third World countries. Their work is frequently unnoticed by the media in the United States, although each volunteer makes a difference in the lives of those they touch. Using the World Wide Web, students will locate Peace Corps members in various locations throughout the world. When tentative contact is made, specific e-mail correspondence will follow. Activities that would enrich this project would be mapmaking, study of the people and culture of the host country, writing, geography, and literature. Students may wish to make and display a world map showing where the Peace Corps volunteers they've contacted are working. Perhaps a future Peace Corps volunteer or diplomat resides in your class.

The Berlin Wall

Following the German defeat after World War II, the city of Berlin was divided into two sections, the Western sector dominated by the Allies and an Eastern sector dominated by the Soviet Union. The final symbol of the division was the construction of the Berlin Wall, which served to separate the people of Germany for three decades.

Objective
Students will make a mural related to their feelings about the Berlin Wall.

Time Required
Two sessions of 1 hour each

Materials
- Internet access
- Library access
- Photos of the wall at different stages of construction
- The famous speech made by President Kennedy by the Berlin Wall in 1963
- Butcher paper
- Crayons, markers, colored pencils

Procedure
Begin with a brief history of the division of Berlin, the Cold War, the construction of the Berlin Wall by the East German government, and the famous "Ich bin ein Berliner" ("I am a Berliner") speech given by President Kennedy in 1963. Have students construct a butcher-paper mural of the Berlin Wall that reflects the feelings and hardships created by this concrete barrier.

Extensions
1. President Kennedy was a Navy hero during World War II when his PT boat (torpedo boat) was destroyed. He led his men to safety and eventual rescue. These qualities were deemed positive for someone who would some day lead his country. What other modern-day Presidents were honored as war heroes?

2. This President and First Lady, Jacqueline Kennedy, entered our homes often via the medium of television. We observed Kennedy in the famous presidential debates, the White House tours, news conferences, and even at the time of the assassination. View some of the Kennedy news tapes to understand his positive presence on camera. Have students watch a television news program for a week, charting all the activities involving the current President.

3. Interview someone who is over fifty years of age and ask where he or she was when President Kennedy was assassinated in Dallas in 1963. What feelings do they remember from that event? Record the comments in a journal, and report back to class.

36th President

Lyndon B. Johnson
1963 - 1969

Lyndon B. Johnson authored more education legislation than any President in history. His background as a teacher may have led him to the belief that education was the only viable vehicle from poverty.

Challenge for Democracy, Listen to History

http://oyez.nwu.edu/
history-out-loud/lbj/

This audio site offers some of President Johnson's Oval Office conversations and speeches to the Joint Session of Congress.

The Lyndon B. Johnson Library and Museum

http://www.lbjlib.utexas.edu/

Administered by the National Archives and Records Administration, this library is a comprehensive text and photo archive site related to the presidency of Lyndon B. Johnson.

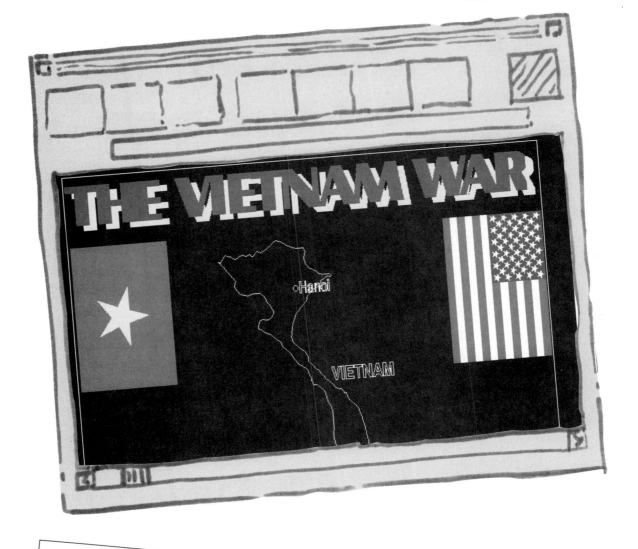

Vietnam War

http://www.bev.net/computer/
htmlhelp/vietnam.html

The Vietnam War history page reviews the murky history of this period. What began as a war to save the world from communism soon became the most divisive conflict since the Civil War. Overshadowing President Johnson's many positive domestic programs, the war tore the country apart, creating mistrust of the military, government, and big business.

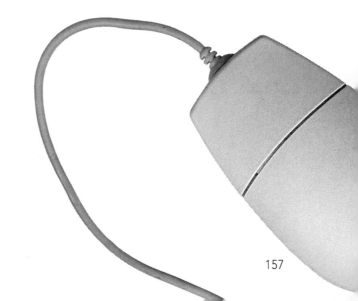

Lessons for Learning

The Great Society

President Johnson sincerely wanted to improve the lives of all Americans. His Great Society program provided funding to improve education, housing, urban development, and hospitalization insurance for the elderly. Among the legislation introduced during his administration were immigration laws, the Voting Rights Act of 1963, and aid to education in disadvantaged urban and rural areas.

Objective
Students will research and report on programs from the President Johnson Great Society initiative.

Time Required
Three sessions of 1 hour each

Materials
• Internet access
• Library resources

Procedure
Have students research various programs from the Great Society, telling how these specific programs made changes in the lives of those who participated in them. Ask each student to tell a story from the perspective of someone who benefited from one of the programs. Students should also judge whether the program was a success and whether any part of it is still in place today.

The Voting Rights Act

The Voting Rights Act of 1965 was designed to protect the voting rights mainly of African Americans. Literacy tests had been developed and implemented for the sole purpose of keeping African Americans from registering to vote. This law made it illegal to use such tests to determine eligibility to vote.

Objective

Students will participate in a simulation of race discrimination caused by discrepancies in voting requirements.

Time Required

1 hour

Materials

- Teacher-created "literacy test"
- Voter registration forms
- Stories from Southern voters prohibited from voting because of race and a literacy test

Procedure

In this simulation, you will design literacy tests. Some of the tests will have questions and phrases much more difficult than the level of the class. None of the students will know that the tests are different and which test is administered to which student. Some students will have to pass the test before they will be eligible to vote in the class election. Some students will be denied the opportunity to vote, while others are given the privilege. The teacher can give the more difficult test to students who are blond or who have short hair or blue eyes. After the election, hold a process feedback exercise to discover how the students felt. Post the comments on the board, and ask students to discuss them, especially comparing this experience to that of the voting literacy tests prior to 1965.

Extensions

1. President Johnson was a teacher before he entered the Congress. Many believe that this background was fundamental to his interest in education and social legislation. What teacher have you had who would make a good President? Why?

2. Johnson was the primary author of the legislation known as the Great Society of the 1960s (a name he gave to his domestic program). If you were President of the United States today, what social issues would you include in the Great Society of the year 2000?

3. In 1964 President Johnson proclaimed a war on poverty with the intention of ending poverty and despair in the United States. Did Johnson accomplish this goal? Do we have poverty today in this country? Provide evidence for your response.

37th President

Richard M. Nixon
1969 - 1974

Although he resigned as President of the United States in 1974, Richard Nixon would later be honored as an effective elder statesman. Perhaps time and history will paint a kinder portrait of this President.

The Facts and Biography

http://www.whitehouse.gov/WH/glimpse/presidents/html/rn37.html

This site reviews both the positive accomplishments of this long-time politician and the negative events that caused a sitting President to resign in disgrace from office. Without question, Nixon's legacy will be remembered and the topic of historians for many years.

Foreign Policy and the Nixon Years

http://www.pbs.org/wgbh/pages/amex/presidents/nf/featured/nixon/nixonfp.html

It may have seemed ironic that the early fighter of communism became the first President to visit the People's Republic of China, a staunch communist stronghold in Asia. Perhaps his efforts in foreign affairs were Nixon's greatest accomplishments. Visit this site and learn more.

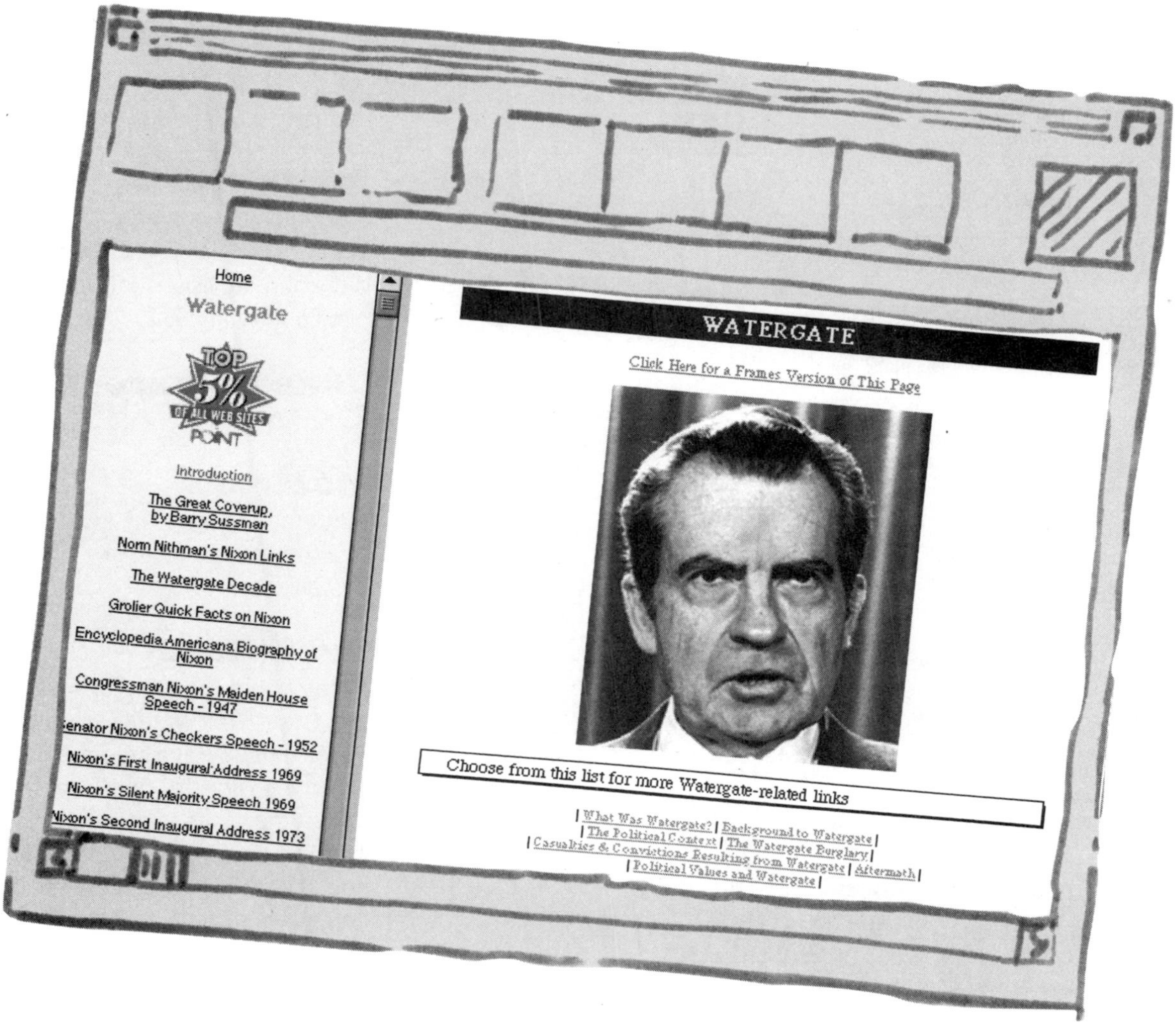

Home
Watergate
TOP 5% OF ALL WEB SITES
POINT
Introduction
The Great Coverup, by Barry Sussman
Norm Nithman's Nixon Links
The Watergate Decade
Grolier Quick Facts on Nixon
Encyclopedia Americana Biography of Nixon
Congressman Nixon's Maiden House Speech - 1947
Senator Nixon's Checkers Speech - 1952
Nixon's First Inaugural Address 1969
Nixon's Silent Majority Speech 1969
Nixon's Second Inaugural Address 1973
WATERGATE
Click Here for a Frames Version of This Page
Choose from this list for more Watergate-related links
| What Was Watergate? | Background to Watergate |
| The Political Context | The Watergate Burglary |
| Casualties & Convictions Resulting from Watergate |
| Political Values and Watergate | Aftermath |

Watergate

http://www.netspace.net.au/~malcolm/wgate.htm

Isn't Watergate a hotel? The word *Watergate* conjures up images of burglary, resignations, presidential disgrace, and public distrust of politicians up to and including the President. This site adds information to the historical events known as "Watergate" that forced the President from elected office.

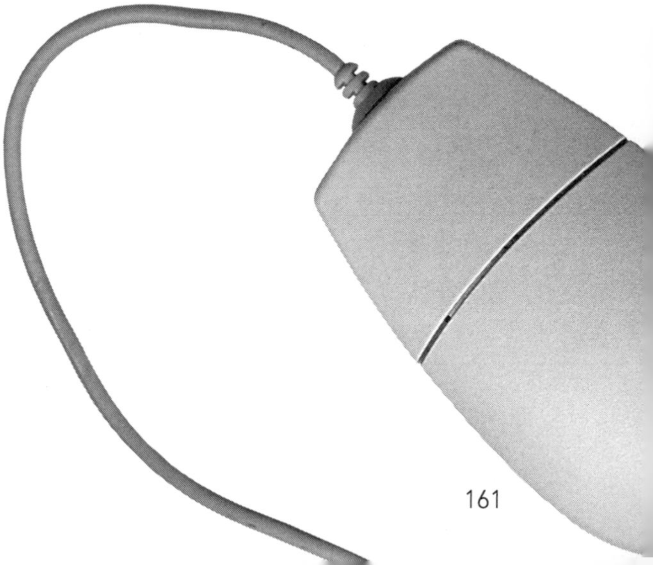

Lessons for Learning

A Walk on the Wall

Objective
Students will walk on the Great Wall of China as President Nixon did when he visited this communist country in 1972.

Time Required
45 minutes

Materials
- Internet access
- Library resources
- Chalk

Procedure
What would it be like to walk on the Great Wall without leaving your school? Have students find the dimensions of the Great Wall. When the width is calculated, have students measure it off on the school yard and draw the outline on the ground. Next, move the entire class to the designated area and see how much of the wall your class would occupy. Given some simple math, calculate the area taken by your students, multiply it by the population of the school, and draw the area needed to hold all the students at your school. Why was the wall constructed so high? Why was it so wide? How long did it take to build?

President Nixon extended the hand of friendship, diplomacy, cultural exchange, and scientific collaboration when he was invited by Chou En-lai to visit the People's Republic of China. His trip signaled a new era in U. S.–Chinese relations. The Great Wall of China has been the backdrop of all presidential visits to China.

A Man on the Moon . . . or Two

Although the space race began during earlier presidential administrations, it was during Nixon's first term as President that Neil Armstrong and Edwin ("Buzz") Aldrin became the first humans to set foot on the moon's surface. By way of the lunar module, the astronauts were able to shuttle from the main spacecraft to the surface of the moon and then return safely back to the mother ship for the journey back to Earth.

Objective
Students will construct their version of the lunar module.

Time Required
1 hour for research
1 hour for construction

Materials
- Internet access
- Egg cartons
- Pipe cleaners
- Foil wrap
- Miscellaneous screws, washers, springs, connectors, etc.

Procedure
Have students search for the lunar module on one of the many moon landing (NASA) World Wide Web sites. After studying the history, operation, and physical characteristics of the module, they will construct their own unique lunar module. At the conclusion, ask students to provide a rational for the construction and use of specific materials. They should name their modules using name stickers and display the modules for all classroom astronauts to view.

Extensions

1. During the Nixon administration, the Twenty-Sixth Amendment to the Constitution was passed and ratified. This amendment gave voting rights to those eighteen years of age and older. Before the ratification of this amendment, citizens had to be twenty-one years old to vote. Discuss why the age was decreased and what the advantages and disadvantages of this action are.

2. Nixon was raised in a Quaker family. Who are the Quakers and what are their beliefs? What interesting conflicts might this create for a President of the United States?

3. Realizing that support for continued military action in Southeast Asia had badly eroded, Nixon began a gradual withdrawal of American troops from the region. Have students identify on a world map and map of Asia the countries most involved in the Vietnam conflict—e.g., Vietnam, Cambodia, Laos, Thailand.

38th President

Gerald R. Ford
1974 - 1977

Gerald Ford, who assumed the reins of the presidency following the resignation of Richard Nixon, would serve his country with honesty and security during a time when both were greatly needed.

Gerald Ford Image Gallery

http://www.ipl.org/ref/POTUS/grford/

A poignant photo page documenting the many moods of the thirty-eighth President.

Gerald R. Ford

http://www.grolier.com/presidents/ea/bios/38pford.html

Gerald Ford is the only person to hold both the office of Vice-President and President who was never elected by the people to either position. The American presidency page on Gerald Ford provides the background and events that led to these and other events in this respected leader's public life.

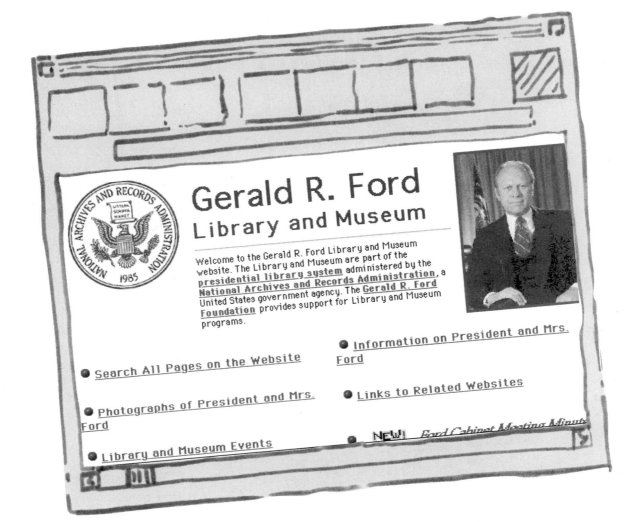

Gerald R. Ford
Library and Museum

Welcome to the Gerald R. Ford Library and Museum website. The Library and Museum are part of the presidential library system administered by the National Archives and Records Administration, a United States government agency. The Gerald R. Ford Foundation provides support for Library and Museum programs.

● Search All Pages on the Website

● Photographs of President and Mrs. Ford

● Library and Museum Events

● Information on President and Mrs. Ford

● Links to Related Websites

● NEW! Ford Cabinet Meeting Minut

The Gerald Ford Library and Museum

http://www.lbjlib.utexas.edu/ford/home page.htm

Welcome to the Gerald Ford Library! Collections, data, text, and photographs make this a rich site of presidential history. Search engines, phone numbers, e-mail addresses, and fax numbers allow the young scholar ample opportunity for further research and study.

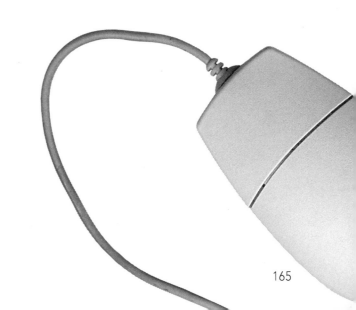

Lessons for Learning

A President Never Elected

Although Gerald Ford was an elected member of Congress, he served as both Vice-President and President of the United States without being elected by the people.

Objective
Students will research and prepare a discussion related to the single individual who became Vice-President and President of the United States without being elected by the people.

Time Required
Two sessions of 1 hour each

Materials
- Internet access
- Library resources
- Writing materials

Procedure
Have students discover through an inquiry process how it was possible for the country to be led by a non-elected President. In addition, have students in cooperative teams present evidence about the issues and problems this creates. This should result in a lively discussion that should continue from the school to the home. Is this an event that could ever happen again?

I Can't Believe It's the Tricentennial

During the presidential term of Gerald Ford, the United States celebrated its two-hundredth birthday, or Bicentennial. In 2076 the Tricentennial will be celebrated, and what a celebration it will be!

Objective
Students will plan the events for the Tricentennial celebration.

Time Required
1 hour

Materials
- Writing materials
- Butcher paper or posterboard
- Crayons, markers, colored pencils

Procedure
Your students can plan this celebration, reflecting upon the past while projecting to the future. Where will we be with technology, health, global conflicts, trade, and population? Will this be a grand party where everyone will come, or one that no one will attend? It is up to your students to plan for this wondrous event.

Extensions
1. Gerald Ford was the first President to make his official health record known to the general public. Was this important? Students can interview a person who has knowledge or an opinion on this topic.

2. When they were young, President Ford played football and President Clinton played the saxophone. Try to discover what hobbies and special interests were associated with other Presidents.

3. First Lady Betty Ford found special causes to embrace. When in our history did the First Lady begin to publicly speak out on social issues and causes? Which other First Ladies have sponsored causes?

39th President

James E. Carter, Jr.
1977 - 1981

James Earl Carter, Jr., who rarely used his proper first name, was known worldwide as Jimmy Carter. He worked hard to improve economic conditions, increase employment, and appoint record numbers of women and other minorities to government jobs. During his presidency, the Department of Education was created.

Camp David Accords: Peace in the Middle East

http://sunsite.unc.edu/sullivan/docs/ CampDavidAccords.html

The Camp David Accords provided a framework for peace between Egypt and Israel. This was an important first step in the long road to securing a lasting peace in a traditionally volatile region.

Jimmy Carter Library

http://redbud.lbjlib.utexas.edu/ carter/home page/home page.htm

Those interested in Jimmy Carter can do their research online at this presidential library site. From the adult stacks to the kid's corner, there's something here for everyone.

Jimmy Carter

(1924 --)

Jimmy Carter (James Earl Carter, Jr.) was born October 1, 1924, in the small farming town of Plains, Georgia. He grew up nearby in the community of Archery. His father, James Earl Carter, Sr., was a farmer and businessman; his mother, Lillian Gordy, a registered nurse. He was educated in the Plains public schools, attended Georgia Southwestern College and the Georgia Institute of Technology, and received a Bachelor of Science degree from the United States Naval Academy in 1946. He later did graduate work in nuclear physics at Union College.

During his naval career he lived in many parts of the United States and served around the world, including the Far East. He rose to the rank of lieutenant (senior grade), working under Admiral Hyman Rickover in the development of the nuclear submarine program.

When his father died in 1953, he resigned his commission and returned to Plains. In addition to working his own farm, he continued a small business of his father's, selling fertilizer and farm supplies. He did the manual labor while his wife Rosalynn

Jimmy Carter

http://sunsite.unc.edu/lia/president/
CarterLibrary/GeneralMaterials/
Biographies/JimmyCarter-bio.html

Jimmy Carter, the son of a peanut farmer, was a nuclear physicist, governor, and then President of the United States. This biographical sketch of the "nickname President" offers a wealth of information.

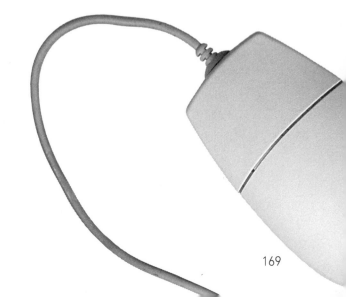

Lessons for Learning

Protest and Change

Early in 1979 a near-disastrous nuclear accident at the Three Mile Island nuclear power plant in Pennsylvania raised national consciousness about the danger of these new sources of domestic power. From a few hundred people at the first protests, to nearly sixty-five thousand people marching on Washington, the protests successfully gained the attention of the government, resulting in a halt to building new facilities and raising the safety standards of those in operation.

Objective

Students will be able to describe the process of protest as it can be used to bring national awareness to a selected cause.

Time Required

Several sessions of 45 minutes each

Materials

- Internet access
- Library resources
- Writing materials
- Newspaper, magazine, and Internet articles
- Photographs

Procedure

Have your students identify a cause about which they can express their desire for change. They may find ideas by reviewing the daily newspaper. The cause may be related to the environment, hunger, care of the aged, gun control, or recycling. It may be local, national, or international in scope.

Have students collect photographs, articles, and other materials related to the cause. Design a large bulletin board in the classroom, hallway, or school cafetorium so that progress on this important social action can be posted and followed by all. Remember, causes gain momentum with publicity and knowledge. Make a difference!

The Department of Energy

Following the oil embargo in the late 1970s, it became apparent that the United States could not rely solely on oil as an energy source. Oil was used not only to power automobiles, but was also used by turbines that generated electricity, by machines in factories, and as the fuel for home and industrial heating. Research began on the development of renewable energy sources, mainly solar, wind, and water.

Objective

Students will be able to describe the need for renewable energy sources as related to the welfare of the United States. Students will be able to design and construct a sample of a solar cooking device.

Time Required

45 minutes

Materials

- Internet access
- Library access
- Pizza box or other flat box
- Aluminum foil
- Cellophane or clear plastic wrap
- Duct tape
- Scissors
- Food to cook

Procedure

In this lesson, students will construct a small solar oven demonstrating the power potential of the sun to cook food and serve as a heat source. Take the cardboard box and cut a large rectangular piece out of the top. Line the inside bottom with foil. Cover the opening with clear plastic wrap using duct tape to secure it in place. Now you should have a box that retains and attracts solar heat.

Lift the lid and place the item you wish to cook on another piece of foil. Students enjoy eating flour tortillas and cheese, or "s'mores" (graham crackers, marshmallows, and pieces of chocolate). Depending on the time of day and the intensity of sunlight and generated heat, you could have a great snack or a melted mess. If you and the kids are in the sun for an extended period of time, be sure to wear sunblock, or you could get cooked too!

Extensions

1. Amy Carter, the President's daughter, was nine years old when she moved into the White House. She attended a Washington public school and often had friends over to play. If you were living in the White House and invited friends to a party, how would you organize it, and what would you serve to eat? Go ahead and have a White House party.

2. President Carter was the first President to be born in a hospital. See if you can discover any of your family or friends who were born in places other than a hospital. Share with the class, and see who has the most unusual birthplace.

3. Jimmy Carter was often referred to as the "Peanut President" because he owned a peanut farm in Plains, Georgia. Good peanut butter is easy to make, since it has only one ingredient—peanuts. Obtain roasted unsalted peanuts in the shell. Shell the peanuts and pour them into a blender. Turn on the blender until the nuts begin to break up and turn to a smooth consistency. The substance will resemble the peanut butter we buy at the store. Add salt if desired, and immediately serve on crackers. Discard any unused portions. Eat and enjoy!

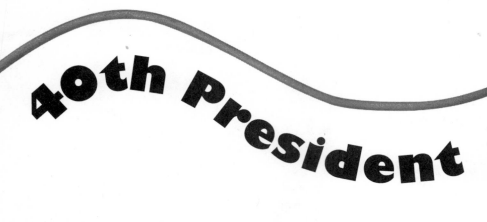

40th President

Ronald W. Reagan
1981 - 1989

A popular actor, union leader, governor, and President, Ronald Reagan appealed to the conservative movement and was respected by world leaders.

The Ronald Reagan Home Page

http://www.dnaco.net/~bkottman/reagan.html

This comprehensive site gives information and insight about our fortieth President as related to the events that occurred during his presidency.

The Challenger Accident

http://www.fas.org/spp/51L.html

The American people had become almost complacent about space shuttle missions. A generation had been born since man had set foot on the moon, and each new launch was only a sound bite on the evening news. But this launch was different. The nation watched as an ordinary schoolteacher and six other astronauts rose into the sky to make history. No one could have imagined what that day would do to our collective memory.

[Text version]

Ronald Reagan

Fortieth President 1981-1989

[Nancy Davis Reagan]

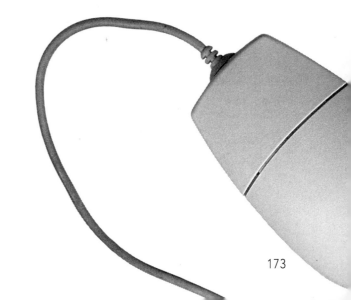

Ronald Reagan

http://www.whitehouse.gov/WH/glimpse/presidents/html/rr40.html

This is the American Dream page, the story of a young boy who grew up in a poor midwestern town, went to college, traveled to Hollywood, and became a movie star. A dream come true, except this young man also was elected governor of California and later President of the United States. Now that's a success story.

Lessons for Learning

From Governor to President

More than one of the Presidents first served as a governor of their state before ascending to the presidency. President Ronald Reagan was one such President.

Objective
Students will be able to describe government organization at both the state level and federal level.

Time Required
Two sessions of 1 hour each

Materials
• Internet access
• Library resources
• Writing materials

Procedure
Reagan was a well-known film actor when he was elected to the governorship of California. As the chief executive of California, he worked with the state assembly and state senate. When he became President of the nation, he was obligated to work closely with members of the U. S. Senate and the House of Representatives. Have students develop a flow chart diagramming how these governmental organizations operate and to what extent they are similar and different.

The Great Communicator

Ronald Reagan was an actor and radio announcer prior to seeking political office. Without question, this experience as a communicator helped him in his rise to political stardom. Many critics accused President Reagan of learning a script rather than understanding the issues. Nonetheless, his ability to communicate and get the message to the people was very effective.

Objective

Students will be able to describe the communications characteristics of this leader, tracing his experience from radio, movies, and politics up to his use of the media as President.

Time Required

Two sessions of 1 hour each

Materials

• Writing materials
• Tape recorder
• Cassette tapes, video clips
• Internet access
• Library access

Procedure

Show video clips of Ronald Reagan in various "performing" roles before he entered politics. Students can then watch speeches and interaction related to his campaign for President and his presidential addresses. Ask students to make assumptions about the similarities of these roles related to communication. Students can then write and record political speeches of their own. They can later be played back and critiqued by members of the class.

Extensions

1. When we borrow money to spend more money than we have, we have personal debt. During the Reagan years, the government spent more than it collected in taxes, thus causing the largest national debt in history. Participate in a simulation to experience how government debt occurs, and find ways to pay off the debt.

2. Following his second term in office and subsequent retirement, Reagan was diagnosed as suffering from Alzheimer's disease. The disclosure of the former President's condition brought about great public awareness of the disease and is resulting in increased research for a cure. Research current information about and definitions of this unfortunate disease.

3. Although the personal computer was actually developed a few years earlier, it was during the Reagan administration that the PC became affordable and available to individuals and small businesses. Apple, IBM, Tandy, Atari, and a host of other computer makers began the information revolution. Your students can try to find some of these early computers (they are still used in many schools) and compare them to the faster and more powerful PCs of today.

41st President

George H. W. Bush
1989 - 1993

George Bush, former Vice-President under Ronald Reagan, offered his "thousand points of light," attempting to ignite national volunteerism and revive a national consciousness.

George Bush Presidential Library

http://www.csdl.tamu.edu/bushlib/bushpage.html

A library of today and tomorrow, the presidential library of George Bush brings together the traditional archives of public papers as well as digital photos of the life of this admired American. Visit this library, museum, and archives to learn more about the forty-first President.

George Bush Biography

http://www.grolier.com/presidents/ea/bios/41pbush.html

President George Bush has a distinguished biography that reads like Who's Who in American service. From a military career, to service in the House of Representatives, Chief of the Central Intelligence Agency, Vice-President, and finally to the highest office in the land, the George Bush Biography site provides the reader with details of greatness.

The Gulf War

http://www.pbs.org/wgbh/pages/frontline/gulf/index.html

A difficult decision was made to respond to Iraq's aggression toward neighboring Kuwait by waging war. This site provides facts about the background, the conflict, censorship, propaganda, and the tragedies of real war.

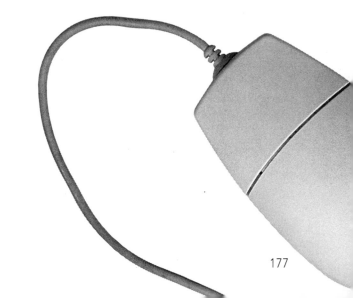

New Government, New Boundaries

For many years, the primary antagonist of the United States was the Soviet Union, composed of many distinct republics. In August 1991, due to major unrest and an attempted coup, the Soviet communist party was dissolved and the U.S.S.R. ceased to exist. In its place were many separate countries that would soon find their names on a new map of the region.

Objective

Students will be able to show the former Soviet Republic while relabeling the classroom map with current boundaries of the independent republics.

Required Time

1 hour

Materials

- Internet access
- Classroom maps (world or former U.S.S.R.)
- Dark permanent-marking pens

Procedure

Classroom maps have become almost a sacred possession hanging from the wall above the chalkboard. Even when new countries have been formed and boundaries have changed, teachers are reluctant to draw new lines on the existing maps.

Many classrooms have maps showing countries that no longer exist or others where the boundaries have been changed for more than twenty-five years. As a wonderful mapping activity, search your maps for needed changes (U.S.S.R., Africa, and the Middle East) and publicly and proudly celebrate the countries by drawing current boundaries on the existing maps. You'll feel a great sense of accomplishment.

History's Worst Environmental Disaster

In March 1989, one of the largest oil spills in history occurred in Alaska's Prince William Sound. The oil tanker *Exxon Valdez* spilled 10 million gallons of oil. The spill covered 4,800 square miles and caused severe environmental and ecological damage.

Objective

Students will be able to describe the events leading to and following the oil spill from the tanker *Exxon Valdez*.

Time Required

Two sessions of 1 hour each

Materials

- Internet access
- Chart paper
- Map of North America
- Butcher paper

Procedure

Utilizing available resources, chart the oil spill, the events, the cleanup, the effect on the physical environment and wildlife, and existing conditions today. Students can use butcher paper to draw the flow of the oil after the disastrous spill. They can indicate the greatest concentration of oil and the greatest loss of animal life and environmental damage.

Following this exercise, students could write letters to the major oil-shipping companies inquiring about what they have done to prevent such disasters from occurring in the future. Students can also make posters emphasizing that people must protect the natural environment. This is a good way of sensitizing young people to their responsibility to protect the environment.

Extensions

1. Following the invasion of Kuwait by the military of Iraq, the United States mobilized its military forces along with those of Britain, Egypt, France, Syria, and a few other countries to overwhelm the invaders and send them back to Iraq. This military action was known as Desert Storm. Students can identify the countries in the region and attempt to rationalize why Iraq wanted to control the oil-rich country of Kuwait.

2. After decades of separation between East and West Germany, the Berlin Wall was torn down. What would you say to someone who had been forced to live behind the Wall for all those years and now was free to experience democracy?

3. President Bush was generally viewed as a good and decent man. During his term as President, he inaugurated a social action program known as "A Thousand Points of Light." The goal was to change society through individuals working for change. Such people became the points of light. Today, meaningful social action is needed as much as ever. Become a point of light by embracing a local social action project.

42nd President

William J. Clinton
1993 –

Bill Clinton, the first "baby-boomer" President, appealed to an aging post-World-War-II population largely because of his age, background, and interests. He and his Vice-President, Al Gore, represented new leadership that was needed to lead the nation into the next millennium.

President Clinton's Trip to Africa

http://www.whitehouse.gov/Africa/

Join the President on this historic trip to a continent where no U. S. President had gone before. A new look at an old continent with a bright future.

Current Occupant: Welcome to the White House

http://www.whitehouse.gov/WH/Welcome.html

This site is almost as good as knocking on the front door, but you don't need to be screened by the Secret Service or have an advance reservation. Participate in the history, the tours, the virtual library, the interactive citizen's handbook, the latest happenings, and even an opportunity to send e-mail.

William Jefferson Clinton

http://www.whitehouse.gov/WH/EOP/
OP/html/OP_Home.html

A product of a troubled home, Clinton achieved his early dreams of becoming President of the United States. A Rhodes scholar at Oxford who later earned a law degree from Yale University, he was a young man on the move. First, he became Arkansas attorney general, and then the nation's youngest governor when elected at the age of thirty-two. He met John Kennedy at the White House and set his sights on the presidency. His journey was completed in 1993. Learn more about this energetic and idealistic national leader in this American presidency biography.

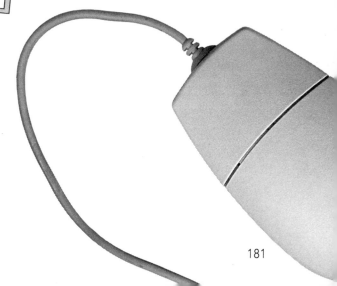

World Wide Web White House

Bill Clinton and Al Gore were the first President and Vice-President to embrace technology, and particularly the Internet, as a tool for personal, business, education, and general communication.

Objective

Students will access the White House via the World Wide Web and follow the activities of the President. Using the daily newspaper online, students will chart the major activities of the President for a period of one week.

Required Time

30 minutes each day for one week

Materials

• Internet access to the White House home page
• Daily newspaper online

Procedure

This administration coined the words "information highway" and offered both fiscal and political support to wire the schools for education in the future. One major highlight of this effort was the creation and development of the White House home page on the World Wide Web. From this page, visitors can tour the White House, visit the president, follow his schedule, view history, and learn about all previous Presidents. Without question, it is a powerful tool.

This technological innovation demonstrates how leadership in a particular area can benefit millions of people.

Instruct students on how to access the World Wide Web by providing instructions on searching or providing the URL, or bookmark the site for easy access. Working in teams, students will follow the President's duties and events,

listing them on a classroom wall chart. To add to this list, students should access one or more of the many online newspapers to search for the daily activities of the President. Following one week of collecting data, ask students to summarize the President's activities and accomplishments. Even a game of golf or a tune on the saxophone is worthy of noting.

The Baby-Boomer President

Bill Clinton was the first President of the United States to be born after World War II. As such, he is part of the "Baby Boomer" generation. Each generation has had music that reflected the political and social climate of the time. This lesson will use the popular music of each decade as an indicator of the mood within the country.

Objective

Students will be able to identify music of the time the President was born, in school, and in the presidency. Students will be able to make critical comments about the music of the period and the political and social times in which the President presided.

Time Required

Two sessions of 1 hour each

Materials

- Internet access
- Chart paper
- Time line
- Music collections from the 1940s through the 1990s

Procedure

Obtain music from each decade from the 1940s through the 1990s. Much of this is on the Internet on various music sites. Have students listen to the music indicative of a particular decade

(just a few samples) and offer assumptions about the political and social climate of the period. Next, the students should check the written history of the time and see if they match. Conclusions can be drawn as to how close music as an art form reflects the mood in society. Students can continue throughout the decades, listing their findings until they arrive at the 1990s and the general prosperity of the Clinton administration. This should be fun, interesting, and certainly an earful.

Extensions

1. Bill Clinton had the opportunity of meeting President John F. Kennedy while he was visiting Washington with the American Legion Boy's Nation Youth Program. He shook hands with the President and from that time decided to pursue a career in politics. Have your students select a person they would like to meet.

2. When the President of the United States travels within the country or around the world, he is transported by *Air Force One*, a huge jet that is transformed into a flying White House. Find out more about this famous plane. Perhaps design the *Air Force One* of the future.

3. Within every era, there are people who have great influence on our

world. During the Clinton years, the names have included Mother Teresa, Princess Diana, and Yitzhak Rabin. Have your students select the influential people whose work coincided with the lives of previous Presidents. This should make for an interesting mix of people and places.

Who's Next?

Just as we cannot be sure if an Internet site will be posted tomorrow, we cannot predict who will become the next President of the United States. Whoever it shall be, man or woman, will be inaugurated as the forty-third U. S. President on the Information Highway.

Election Night Record

This space is provided for your students to begin to gather data on the candidates for the next presidential election. They can make predictions and keep track of the primary and national elections. They can note those who drop out of the race and those who continue. They can begin to develop the biography of the front runners, the time we live in, and the events that are occurring. Go online to the Web pages that will be developed for each candidate. Your students will write the next chapter of this book. In a short time, you will know the next President of the United States.

_____

_____

_____

_____

_____

_____

_____

_____

_____

_____

_____

_____

_____

_____

Resources, Journals and Organizations, and Other Places

The following resources may be of interest or use to you. The resources will only grow, so keep adding to the list as you travel. Contact any of these resources for connections to others.

America Online
Commercial Service
1-800-827-3338

The authors' e-mail:
gmgarfield@csupomona.edu
smcdono@cyberg8t.com

Classroom Prodigy
2364 Harcourt
San Diego, CA 92123

CUE/Journal
Computer Using Educators Inc.
1210 Marina Village Parkway,
Suite 100
Alameda, CA 94501
http://www.cue.org

Custom Computers for Kids
3 Oak Forest Road
Novato, CA 94949

Educational Leadership
Journal of the Association for
Supervision and Curriculum
Development
1250 N. Pitt Street
Alexandria, VA 22314

Kappan
Phi Delta Kappa
P.O. Box 789
Bloomington, IN 47402-9961

MacWAREHOUSE Catalogue
P.O. Box 3013
1720 Oak Street
Lakewood, NJ 08701-3013
1-800-255-6227

Net Guide
P. O. Box 420355
Palm Crest, FL 32142-9371

Professional Teaching Associates
Educational Technology
Consultants for Classroom
Teachers
1053 Alamosa Drive
Claremont, CA 91711

Teacher Magazine
P.O. Box 2090
Marion, OH 43306

Teaching K–8
40 Richards Avenue
Norwalk, CT 06854

Yahoo Internet Life
P.O. Box 53380
Boulder, CO 80322

Government Web sites:

Library of Congress
http://lcweb.loc.gov/homepage/lchp.html

The White House
http://www.whitehouse.gov/

The Smithsonian Institution
http://www/si.edu/

Acknowledgements

Adams, John. *The White House Collection,* copyright White House Historical Association.
Adams, John Quincy. Reprinted by permission of Robert S. Summers, Internet Public Library, http://ipl.org.
Arthur, Chester A. Reprinted by permission of Paul Silhan. All rights reserved.

Buchanan, James. Courtesy of The James Buchanan Foundation for the Preservation of Wheatland, Lancaster, PA.

Carter, Jimmy. Reprinted courtesy of The President Project, Leadership Information Archives, UNC Chapel Hill.
Cleveland, Grover. Site reprinted by permission of Josh Smith. E-mail: db_3@hotmail.com.
Clinton, William Jefferson. Courtesy of the White House Historical Association.
Cuban Missile Crisis. Website developed by Ben Larson and Kurt Wiersma in the spirit of informing and enlightening students, teachers, and citizens around the globe.
<http://library.advanced.org/11046/7>

Garfield, James A. Source:
http://www.peoples.net/southbd/pres19.html.
Grant, Ulysses S. Reprinted courtesy of Candace Scott.
Gulf War. The Gulf War web site is one of Frontline's many web sites which go with each Frontline documentary report. Reprinted by permission of PBS.

Harding, Warren G. *The White House Collection,* copyright White House Historical Association.
Harrison, William H. Courtesy of Project Bartleby Archive.
Hayes, Rutherford B. Reprinted courtesy of the R. B. Hayes Presidential Center, Fremont Ohio. Design by Gilbert Gonzalez.
Hoover, Herbert. Courtesy of the Hoover Library.

Jackson, Andrew. Courtesy of The Hermitage.

Johnson, Andrew. Source:
http://www.peoples.net/pres16.html.

Lincoln, Abraham. Reprinted by permission of The History Place, www.historyplace.com.
Lindbergh, Charles. Reprinted by permission of the National Air and Space Museum — Smithsonian Institution.

Madison, James. James Madison bust by Ken Bear. Reprinted by permission of James Madison University Department of Political Science.
McKinley, Wm. Courtesy of Ohio State University Department of History.
Monroe, James. Reprinted courtesy of Thomas E. Gort.
Montgomery Bus Boycott. Image courtesy of the collection of The National Civil Rights Museum, Memphis, Tennessee.
Monticello. Courtesy of Monticello/Thomas Jefferson Memorial Foundation, Inc.

Netscape. Portions Copyright Netscape Communications Corporation, 1998. All Rights Reserved. Netscape, Netscape Navigator and the Netscape N Logo, are registered trademarks of Netscape in the United States and other countries.

Panama Canal. Courtesy of the Panama Canal Commission.
Pierce, Franklin. *The White House Collection,* copyright White House Historical Association.

Reagan, Ronald. *The White House Collection,* copyright White House Historical Association.
Roosevelt, Franklin Delano. Site reprinted courtesy of the Access Indiana Information Network. Photo from *The White House Collection,* copyright White House Historical Association.

Taft, Wm. Howard. *The White House Collection,* copyright White House Historical Association.
Taylor, Zachary. Reprinted by permission of Robert S. Summers, Internet Public Library, http://ipl.org.
Truman, Harry S. Reprinted courtesy of the Harry S. Truman Library.
Tyler, John. Reprinted courtesy of Sherwood Forest. Photo by Greg Hadley Photography.
Tyler, John. Reprinted by permission of Robert S. Summers, Internet Public Library, http://ipl.org.

U.S. - Mexican War. Reprinted courtesy of the Descendants of Mexican War Veterans.

van Buren, Martin. Courtesy of Project Bartleby Archive.
Vietnam War. Source: www.bev.net/computer/htmlhelp/vietnam.html.

Washington, George. Reprinted courtesy of the Papers of George Washington, http://www.virgina.edu/gwpapers/.
Watergate. Courtesy of Malcolm Farnsworth.
White House. Courtesy of the White House Historical Association.
Wounded Knee. Site reprinted by permission of Jordan S. Dill (www.dickshovel.com). Image reprinted by permission of Frank Howell, Inc. (www.rt66.com/~bluraven/).